Roger Shenton

CHANGING TRACKS

The photographs
of a midlands railwayman
1946 to 1994

Former LMSR 'Jubilee' class 4-6-0 No 45617 *Mauritius*,
takes the Northampton line out of Rugby Midland,
with the 09.10 Llandudno to London Euston
on 1st April 1954.

Title page photograph:
Former LMSR 'Patriot' class 4-6-0
No 45538 *Giggleswick* moves at reduced speed
over a temporary drainage restriction with an
up fast fitted freight, near Grendon,
at WCML 103$^{1}/_{2}$ mp, on 9th April 1960.
Originally built as LNWR 'Claughton' No15, it
was numbered 6000 when rebuilt at Crewe
in 1933, then renumbered No 5538 in 1934.
It was named at Settle Station in 1938,
after the local public school
and was withdrawn in September 1962.

Roger Shenton

CHANGING TRACKS

The photographs
of a midlands railwayman
1946 to 1994

Midland Publishing
Limited

To my wife June
as some recompense
for the years she has had to endure
my addiction to railways,
and to our children Anne and Richard,
who have chosen to follow their parents
into railway careers.

© Roger Shenton
1995

Published by
Midland Publishing Limited
24 The Hollow, Earl Shilton
Leicester, LE9 7NA
England

ISBN 1 85780 004 4

Design concept and layout
© Midland Publishing Limited
and Stephen Thompson Associates.

Typeset in
ITC Garamond and Gill Sans

Printed in England by
Hillman Printers (Frome) Limited
Frome, Somerset

I wish to express
my sincere thanks to Colin Ainsworth,
Jim Peden and Brian Stead
for their assistance with compiling
caption data.

INTRODUCTION

I WAS BORN to a non-railway family living in a farm cottage near the hamlet of Streethay, about ½ mile east of Lichfield Trent Valley station. The sounds of a steady stream of ex-London & North Western 'Super D' 0-8-0s and Midland 3Fs plodding towards the Black Country with goods trains from Wichnor sidings were enough to instil a lifelong love of railways in an infant. My parents acknowledged this interest and an early snapshot reproduced here, shows me astride a wooden 6-coupled model of LNER A4 Pacific *Silver Link,* which our old dog *Buffin* used to pull along the garden paths at home. My first 'real' locomotive came in the shape of a second hand Bassett-Lowke clockwork '0' gauge model of a LMS 'Compound' 4-4-0. Perhaps this is what led me to have a particular affinity in later life for full sized 4-4-0s.

I have never been one to concentrate for long on things which failed to hold my interest and unfortunately for my mother, school work came into this category. School days in wartime provided many opportunities to avoid academic study, from potato picking on local farms in the autumn to postal deliveries at Christmas, through numerous Army or Air Force cadet courses. I took every chance I had to play truant, learning more about the rules and regulations which governed railway signalling, from the many visits I made to local signal boxes, than those subjects I was supposed to study at school.

Among the vivid memories I have from those days are the frequent comings and goings of special trains conveying US troops to military barracks in the Lichfield area in the build up towards D-Day and of one very special event at Lichfield Trent Valley station when on the afternoon of 20th June 1944 the Mayor performed the naming ceremony on the new LMS Stanier 'Pacific' No 6250 *City of Lichfield*. I witnessed this event from a vantage point on top of the railings of the cattle pen nearby. Little did I think that 30 years later, I would be one of the official party witnessing Lady Leonora, Countess of Lichfield, performing the ceremony to unveil the same name on AC electric locomotive No 86 207.

Cycle rides to places further afield were undertaken during school holidays. A popular destination was Wolverhampton where I used to stand against the railings above the canal towpath where the Great Western Railway's main line through Dunstall Park passed the coaling plant and turntable road leading to and from Stafford Road shed.

From this spot an eye could also be kept upon the Stour Valley line viaduct for trains running between Bushbury and Wolverhampton High Level station. For example on 11th October 1947 a total of 70 GWR locomotives were 'spotted' in a 6-hour period. These included 3 'Kings', 11 'Castles', 3 'Stars', 3 'Counties', 11 'Halls' and 5 'Granges'. In the same period 28 LMSR engines were recorded including 2 'Jubilees', 2 'Royal Scots' and 4 'Patriots'.

It is but a short step from spotting to photography. My first attempts to capture trains on film started in 1946 when I borrowed my mother's old Kodak Box Brownie, retrieved from the wardrobe after the war years and dusted off. Film had been virtually unobtainable during the war but chemists' shops were now selling ex-War Department 120 rolls. These came in sealed envelopes made of black greaseproof paper. The quality of these was variable and several of my pre-nationalisation photographs were ruined by the appearance of a horizontal line running through the entire negative. It was impossible to record trains in motion using such primitive equipment though matters much improved when I bought a second-hand Kodak Retina 35mm camera in 1952.

The inevitable happened and I went straight from school to work on the railway. My first job was in the booking and parcels office at Lichfield Trent Valley Station. Travel beyond one's locality was still the exception rather than the rule. As bus and train services out of Lichfield were non existant on Sundays until after noon, on many occasions, with my friend Jeff Webb, I would cycle the 16 miles to Birmingham, to join one of the Stephenson Locomotive Society railtours organised by the late W A 'Cam' Camwell.

This book is the manifestation of my lifelong interest in railways and is a photographic reflection on how the railway scene has changed in the 45 years or so since I began work for BR. When considering what material I wished to include in this book the question of how the photographs should be presented required considerable thought. The idea of dividing the pictures up into regions, routes or locomotive types did not appeal to me. I have therefore presented the pictures in date order, rather like a diary or a scrapbook as I think this best reflects the changes which have occurred, and which I have been able to both observe and record, over the years.

When I began taking pictures in the years before nationalisation, the railways of the midlands were virtually 100% steam operated, the only exceptions to steam power being a few GWR railcars and LMSR diesel shunters. Most stations were unchanged since they had been built in the last century; some still had three classes of waiting rooms. Semaphore signalling was the rule, only some distant signals on main routes were colour lights. The track in use consisted largely of bullhead rail laid on wooden sleepers. Flat bottomed rail was only to be found in isolated stretches on some main lines and continuous welded rail was still very much in the future. Track maintenance was a labour intensive business, mostly conducted by locally based permanent way gangs.

The industrial railway still flourished. The bulk of freight traffic went by rail and at sites all over the midlands factory sidings with steam locomotives to shunt them, were to be found. Collieries operated a great variety of steam locomotives. These ranged from some of the vintage machines at work around the coalfields on Cannock Chase in Staffordshire, to new locomotives purchased by the National Coal Board for pits in various parts of the region and the highly polished saddle tanks operated by the breweries, constantly to be seen trundling across the many level crossings in Burton-on-Trent.

The 1950s saw an influx of BR's Riddles-designed standard locomotives. Whilst the arrival of these meant that some old favourites had their services dispensed with, the sight of diesel locomotives like the 'Fell', the prototype 'Deltic' and the pair of main line diesel electrics built by Ivatt at Derby in 1947/8 for the LMSR/BR, were still very much novelties, rather than the advance guard of the new regime. The first inroads of dieselisation came with the arrival of diesel multiple units (DMUs) for branch, suburban and cross-country line services.

The closure, in March 1959, of the former Midland & Great Northern system, which linked the east midlands to the east coast, was a melancholy harbinger of the massive closure of stations, branch lines and indeed some main routes like the Great Central line to London and the GWR line north of Birmingham, which were to come in the 1960s and '70s. Many of the closures initiated by the infamous Dr Beeching and his successors were so terribly short-sighted. The continental loading gauge of the old GCR would be very useful now that Britain's railways are linked to those of Europe through the Channel Tunnel, whilst less than 20 years after the closure of the GWR station at Snow Hill in Birmingham, a new Snow Hill has risen on its site.

Today the railway has indeed radically changed from that which I observed as a boy and worked on as a young man. Many motive power depots have closed along with many of the lines for which they provided locomotives. Multiple aspect colour light signals controlled from power signal boxes have replaced many of the old mechanical boxes and the semaphores which they operated. Many of the Victorian stations have been replaced with bus-stop type waiting shelters. The permanent way is maintained by mobile gangs who travel in specially built road vehicles – their work having been revolutionised through the application of much specialised machinery and the widespread introduction of continuous welded rail.

Steam has disappeared, except on the preserved lines and on the occasional main line special. The coal industry has suffered a drastic contraction as has much of the heavy industry which once supported its own private railway systems in the region. On the positive side new stations have been opened and passenger services have been restored to sections of line which lost them in the closures of the Beeching era.

I have tried to give a railwayman's perspective on the changes of the last four decades. I hope the photographs will revive memories for older readers and perhaps provide some insight, for those not so old, into what the railway scene was like and how it has changed, in the years covered by the book. I would also like to think that the captions to the photographs will impart some information which will jog the memory, and complement my purpose in setting out to write this book in the first place, which has been to record how the tracks have changed in the years in which I have known them.

Roger Shenton,
Pelsall   June 1995

Lichfield Trent Valley

LMS 2-6-0 No 2973, built at Crewe Works in 1934, stands on the up slow. It was one of 40 of a class which was Stanier's first tender engine design for the LMSR. No 2973 has had to draw past the stop signal to get its lengthy train clear of the up fast, off the two-track section north of Lichfield No 2 Signal Box, to await a path over the two-track section to Tamworth. The length of such freights necessitated the use of a 'calling on' arm to bring trains clear of the up fast line. The large gantry in the picture was split a year or so later and a new slow line gantry was positioned in advance of where the locomotives are in the picture. The daily local pick-up goods to Burton-on-Trent, headed by 4-4-0 No 364, which was built at Derby in 1886 and rebuilt in 1923, has its train made up and ready for departure.
21st September 1946

Lichfield Trent Valley Station

LMS 4-6-0 'Patriot' class No 5526 stands in the up platform with a local passenger train. Built originally at Crewe works as a 'Claughton' class locomotive to a Bowen-Cooke design and given the LNWR number 972, it became LMS No 5963 after the grouping in 1923. Transformation to the 'Patriot' class took place at Derby works in 1933. It was renumbered 5526 in 1934 and named *Morecambe & Heysham* in 1937. A final rebuild took place at Crewe in 1947 when a 2A boiler was fitted, giving it a higher power classification of 6P. Withdrawal from BR service took place in 1964. A train destined for Burton-on-Trent can be observed at the High Level Station above the 'Patriot'.
28th September 1946

Derby Motive Power Depot (17A)

Above: Ex-Midland Railway, S W Johnson-designed 0-6-0 No 2992 was built at the Derby Works in the 1870s. In excess of 900 were built and all went into the LMSR stock. At nationalisation in 1948, 600-odd were still in service. Originally classed 2F, some were reboilered and reclassified 3F. Those remaining as 2Fs were renumbered in the 58000 series whilst the 3Fs had the prefix '4' added to their LMS numbers in line with the BR renumbering practice for ex-LMSR locomotives. *24th July 1947*

Derby Motive Power Depot (17A)

Above: Ex-Midland Railway 0-4-0T No 1537 was built at Derby Works in 1922. Designed by R M Deeley, 10 were built between 1907 and 1922, all being taken into BR stock in 1948. They were used mainly in brewery and steel works exchange sidings where their short wheelbase was ideal for coping with the tight curves regularly encountered there. *6th February 1948*

Lichfield Trent Valley Station

Above: An up local passenger train stands clear of the bridge, which carried the platforms of the High Level Station. LMS class 5 No 4941, was one of a batch of 12 'Black 5's (Nos 4932-4943) built in 1945 at the former Lancashire & Yorkshire Railway Works at Horwich. The covered stairway, seen to the right of the picture, led from the up Trent Valley line platform, to the up South Staffs platform. *25th March 1948*

Gnosall

Right: An extremely rare Shropshire Union warning notice displayed at an overbridge west of the village. The Shopshire Union Railway built the line between Wellington and Stafford. Opened in 1849, it was later absorbed into the LNWR. Closure to passenger traffic came in September 1964 and freight ceased beyond Donnington in 1966. *2nd June 1948*

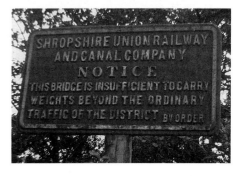

Lichfield Trent Valley Station

Above: The 11.40 Liverpool Lime Street to Rugby 'Class A' passenger is in the charge of one of the last three unrebuilt 'Royal Scot' class 4-6-0 locomotives, No 6148 *The Manchester Regiment*. Built under contract by the North British Locomotive Company in Glasgow at their Hyde Park Works in 1927, it was originally named *Velocipede* but was renamed in the mid-1930s. Rebuilding with a 2A taper boiler took place in July 1954 and it was withdrawn from service in December 1964. *26th March 1948*

Centre left: The driver walks around the ex-LNWR 4-6-0 No 25648 *Queen of the Belgians*, working the 17.20 Nuneaton Trent Valley to Stafford local passenger. It was originally built at Crewe Works to a Bowen-Cooke design, as LNWR No 2396. The class, which originally totalled 246 locomotives, was built between 1911 and 1921. Of these, only four survived to be taken into BR stock in 1948 (Nos 25648, 25673, 25752 and 25787). Although allocated BR numbers 58000-3, none lasted long enough to carry them, all being withdrawn in 1949. *7th May 1948*

Saltley Motive Power Depot (21A)

Lower left: The No 2 roundhouse contains amongst others, Stanier 8F 2-8-0 No 8635, built at Brighton works in 1943 and allocated to Nottingham (16A); Class 5 4-6-0 No 4920, built at Crewe Works in 1945; and ex-Midland Railway 4-4-0 No 493, an S W Johnson design, built in 1897 and subsequently rebuilt by both Deeley and Fowler. The shed lost its roof during air raids; replacement took place shortly prior to closure! *6th June 1948*

Saltley Motive Power Depot (21A)

Right: Originally designed by Matthew Kirtley, this double framed 0-6-0 No 22853 was built at Derby Works in 1874. Produced in extremely large numbers from 1863 to 1874, these locomotives underwent various rebuildings during their long working lives. This photograph shows the locomotive carrying a Johnson cab and boiler fittings, but retaining its Kirtley tender. No 2853 became LMSR 22853 in the 1930s and was one of only four to pass into BR ownership. Although allocated the number 58112, it was scrapped before it could carry it. They were used mainly on the Halesowen branch in their last years at Saltley. *6th June 1948*

Lichfield Trent Valley Station

Bottom: Due to engineering works between Wichnor Junction and Kingsbury Junction on the Midland line from Birmingham to Derby, through Tamworth High Level Station, a shuttle service was being run along the Trent Valley line from Tamworth to Lichfield, at this time. Passengers from Tamworth bound for the north-east or south-west could thus join their diverted expresses at Lichfield Trent Valley High Level Station. The LMSR introduced this class of mixed traffic 2-6-0 Mogul in 1947, to the design of H G Ivatt, and No 43023 was the first of 27 produced in 1949 at Horwich Works. The twin-orifice blastpipe and double chimney did not stay long with the class due to poor steaming: replacement with a single chimney solved the problem. *19th March 1949*

Crewe North Motive Power Depot (5A)

Right: LMS 'Royal Scot' class 4-6-0 No 46130 rests between turns. This was one of the 25 (Nos 6125-49) built under contract by the North British Locomotive Company at their Hyde Park Works in 1927. Originally named *Liverpool,* this was changed to *The West Yorkshire Regiment* in 1935-6. Rebuilding with a Stanier 2A taper boiler took place in 1949, and withdrawal from service came in December 1962. Although the locomotive has had its new BR number applied, the tender still displays allegiance to its former owner, the LMSR. *27th November 1948*

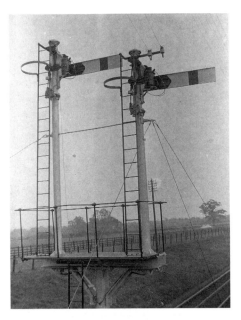

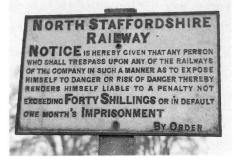

Stone Station

Above: North Staffordshire Railway notice displayed by a wicket gate, at the south end of the down platform, where the tracks cross a public footpath. *11th October 1950*

Armitage – WCML

Top left: New down outer home signal gantry erected at 120¾ mp. The height of the arms was reversed on 17th December 1961 to signify the transposing of the down fast and slow lines between Armitage and Colwich Junction. These were replaced when multiple aspect signalling was introduced on 9th July 1962. *6th September 1949*

Bottesford North Junction

Top centre: Great Northern Railway trespass and warning notices dated July 1896. *21st February 1950*

Brixworth Station

Far left: London North Western Railway weight restriction notices, painted red with white lettering. *10th August 1950*

Worcester Foregate Street Station

Centre right: Great Western Railway blue and white enamel tresspass notice contained in a frame. *29th June 1949*

Lichfield Trent Valley Station

Left: LMSR rebuilt 'Patriot' class 4-6-0 No 45536 *Private W. Wood V.C.* stands with the 08.20 Manchester London Road to London Euston express. Both this locomotive and No 5537 *Private E. Sykes V.C.* received names in 1926 commemorating railway employees who were awarded the ultimate decoration for gallantry in the 1914-1918 war. Wilfred Wood, a retired foreman from Longsight MPD, died aged 84, in 1982. No 45536 was built as one of Bowen-Cooke's 'Claughton' class locomotives in 1920 for the LNWR. It became LMS No 6018 at grouping. Renumbered 5536 in 1934, it was rebuilt in 1933 and again in 1948. Windshields, (smoke deflectors) were later added to the smokebox sides. No 45536 was withdrawn by BR in 1962. *14th April 1949*

Lichfield Trent Valley

Above: Newly constructed 0-4-0ST, (works No 2961) named *NCB Chislet No 2,* has been stopped with a hot axle box *en route* to Chislet Colliery in the Kent coalfield from Bagnall's works at Stafford. *30th June 1950*

Lichfield Trent Valley Station

Right: The up side station garden was wedged between the up slow platform line and the down branch (from the High Level Junction). Second prize was awarded in the annual 'Best Kept Garden' competition organised by the Rugby District Operating Superintendant. Porter Vic Cowlishaw is seen attending the blooms. *5th July 1951*

Lichfield Trent Valley No 1 Signal Box

Below: Members of the staff on the signalbox steps, standing Albert Smith (Shunter) with Jack Pritchard (Signalman) and seated Roy Biggin (Train Recorder) above Leslie Eaton (Relief Signalman). At this time there were 43 staff on the payroll at this station. *23rd September 1951*

Gailey Station

Above: Opened to passengers on the Grand Junction Railway in July 1837 with the name of Spread Eagle, renamed Gailey in August 1881, and closed in June 1951. The platforms remained until May 1962 when they were removed to make way for electrification works. The buildings are now a private residence. *18th June 1951*

Hademore Crossing – 113½ mp WCML

Above: One of the first ballast cleaning machines, numbered BC 29, is working on the up line, south of the crossing, on the West Coast main line. The machine weighed 11 tons 5 cwt and achieved a working rate of 80 yards per hour. Movement was achieved by securing a wire rope ahead of the machine to a sleeper and winching it in on the drum, to the left of the seated operator. The track has been jacked up to allow the cutter bar to collect ballast and deposit it into the wagons alongside. *23rd March 1952*

Worcester Shrub Hill Station

Left: An ex-GWR 'Star' class No 4021 *British Monarch*, designed by G J Churchward and introduced in 1907, stands in the up platform. Note the high pitched screw reverser giving no room for a driver's seat. Until 1927 No 4021 was named *King Edward*. It lost this name when the 'King' class was introduced in that year. The 'Star' is seen here on an Hereford to Paddington express. *7th April 1952*

Lichfield Trent Valley High Level Station

Above: Former LMSR class 4 2-6-0 No 43119, built at Horwich works in 1951, working an excursion from Lincoln to Dudley. These excursions from the East Midlands to Dudley, for the zoo and castle, were very popular throughout the 1950s. Every Bank Holiday as many as eight trains were run, made up from scratch stock and 'borrowed' locomotives in many cases. *13th April 1952*

Knowle & Dorridge Station

Left: Ex-GWR 'King' class 4-6-0 No 6018 *King Henry VI* working the 09.10 London Paddington to Birkenhead Woodside. This locomotive would be replaced at Wolverhampton Low Level due to an axle-load restriction of 22½ tons, further north. *19th May 1952*

Liverpool Exchange Station

Right: The 14.15 to Glasgow headed by BR Standard class 6MT 4-6-2 No 72001 *Clan Cameron*, built at Crewe in December 1951 and withdrawn in December 1962 from Polmadie depot, Glasgow, and scrapped at Darlington Works. *26th May 1952*

Birmingham New Street Station

Below: One of F W Webb's 0-6-2 tanks, of which over 300 were built at Crewe between 1881 and 1896, numbered 3724 by the LNWR, it became LMS No 7699. This was one of 64 taken into BR stock. Bearing its BR No 58900, it is at work as the western (LNWR) side pilot. No 58926, LNWR No 1054, has been preserved. *19th May 1952*

Lichfield Trent Valley – 116½ mp WCML

Right: LMS-designed and built in 1947, Co-Co 1600 hp diesel electric locomotive No 10000 is seen here heading the 10.10 'Class A' Blackpool Central to London Euston passenger. The LMS raised aluminium letters have been removed but the figures remain. The locomotive was withdrawn from service in March 1966 and was cut up for scrap by Cashmores at Great Bridge around 1968. *6th July 1952*

Lichfield Trent Valley Station

Above: The 11.50 'Class A' London Euston to Crewe and Birmingham. The rear portion was detached at Rugby and worked forward to Birmingham by a Rugby locomotive. The double-headed train is piloted by unrebuilt 'Royal Scot' class No 46134 *The Cheshire Regiment*, built in 1927 by the North British Loco Company and originally named *Atlas*. Names were changed during the 1935/6 period and rebuilding with a 2A taper boiler took place in 1953. This locomotive was withdrawn in December 1962. The second locomotive, ex-LMS 'Royal Scot' 46136 *The Border Regiment*, originally named *Goliath*, was rebuilt in March 1950 and withdrawn in March 1964. The train, incidentally, was composed of only five vehicles, an average loading for this service. *7th July 1952*

Buxton Station

Above: Former Midland Class 1P 0-4-4T, built at Derby in 1899 as No 1421, is working the Miller's Dale shuttle service. The locomotive is carrying its BR number 58084 Passenger services between Buxton and Miller's Dale ceased on 6th March 1967. *8th July 1952*

Burton-on-Trent Station

Opposite page, top: The 20.05 departure for Bristol awaits the 'right away' headed by ex-LMS 'Patriot' class 4-6-0 No 45524 *Blackpool*, rebuilt from LNWR 'Claughton' No.1319 in 1933 at Crewe Works. The LMS number 5907 allocated to this locomotive at grouping in 1923 was changed to No 5524 in 1934 and the original name *Sir Frederick Harrison* was changed in 1936. This locomotive was never given a taper boiler and remained in the condition seen here until its withdrawal in 1962. This view, looking west, shows the Walsall bay track with exit signals to the right of the loco; beyond the signal gantry to the right of the picture is the Motive Power Depot, which closed in 1966, and Burton Station south box, rendered redundant in June 1969 with the introduction of multiple aspect signalling operated from Derby power signal box. *8th July 1952*

Lichfield Trent Valley Station

Above: A view taken from a window in No 1 Signal Box of ex-LMSR 'Patriot' class 4-6-0 No 45503 *The Royal Leicestershire Regiment*, working the 11.50 London Euston to Crewe. Originally LNWR 'Claughton' class

No 808, this locomotive was rebuilt at Crewe Works in 1932 and carried its original LMS No 5985 until the renumbering scheme of 1934 when it became No 5503. Its name from 1938, *The Leicestershire Regiment*, was amended in 1948 to include the word 'Royal'. No 45503 was withdrawn

in August 1961, in this condition, not having received the 2A taper boiler. This view shows not only the air vents protruding from the coal, but the open tank filler cap and fire irons scattered across the top of the tender. *21st July 1952*

Nottingham Victoria Station

Above: Ex-LNER K3 class 2-6-0 No 61977 approaches the North signal box heading towards Mansfield Road tunnel. Victoria Station was opened by the Great Central Railway in May 1900 and finally closed in September 1967. The site is now a shopping centre. *2nd August 1952*

Nottingham Midland Station

Left: LMSR 2-6-0 No 46443, built at Crewe Works in 1950 and now preserved on the Severn Valley Railway, stands on the scissors crossing beside No 2 platform having worked in the 14.40 local passenger train from Derby. Through passenger services ceased in September 1966 *2nd August 1952*

Lichfield Trent Valley Station

Below left: Class 5MT 4-6-0 No 44777, built at Crewe Works in 1947, her tender still lettered 'LMS', hauls sister loco No 44822, built at Derby in 1944, to Crewe Works. The bell attached to No 1 Signal Box was rung to warn platform staff of an approaching train booked to stop. *14th August 1952*

Rugby Central Station

Opposite page, bottom: Former LNER 2-8-0 O1 class No 63868 enters the up loop to allow a following Marylebone express to pass. Introduced by Edward Thompson in 1944, these were rebuilds of some of the locomotives of the O4 Class, which dated back to 1911 when they were designed for the Great Central Railway by Robinson. This machine lacks vacuum brakes, carries a three link front coupling and retains the distinctive high capacity tender favoured by the Railway Operating Department in the First World War. *22nd September 1952*

Lichfield Trent Valley

Top right: The 11.40 'Class A' Liverpool Lime Street to Rugby had departed from Rugeley Trent Valley shortly after 14.00 hrs, when, passing Armitage signal box the signalman noticed smoke coming from inside the leading coach. Stop and Examine (7 bells) was immediately sent over the telegraph to Elmhurst Crossing, the next box. Stopped out of course, the enginemen soon realised the problem. The guard moved passengers from the burning vehicle, brake third corridor (BTK) W4646, through the corridor connection before the fireman uncoupled the engine and burning coach from the remainder of the train. This scene shows the engine, LMS 'Black 5' No 44773, built at Crewe works in 1947, arriving on the up slow line, where the local fire brigade dealt with the blaze. *23rd August 1952*

Lichfield Trent Valley No 2 Signal Box

Centre right: Stabled former GWR BTK (third class was not redesignated second until 3rd June 1956) No W4646 awaits disposal. The coach was built at Swindon Works in October 1923 as part of Lot 1332. During the Second World War it formed part of an ambulance train. An inquiry assumed a spark from the locomotive had entered an open window causing the fire. A quantity of parcels and letter mail was destroyed. *24th August 1952*

Derby Works

Above: Johnson 0-4-0ST No 41523, built at Derby Works in 1903, stands with 3-cylinder 'Compound' 4-4-0 No 40900, originally built for the LMS in 1927 at the Vulcan Foundry in Newton-le-Willows. The 25 'Compounds', Nos 1160 to 1184, constructed there in 1925, were followed by another 40, Nos 900 to 924 and 1185 to 1199 in 1927. *28th September 1952*

Centre left: Johnson introduced his 4-4-0 Class 3P design in 1900 and 80 locomotives were built up to 1905. Twenty-two survived to enter BR ownership. Here Nos 40743 and 40728 from the final batch built at Derby in 1903 and 1902 respectively, await the cutter's torch. *28th September 1952*

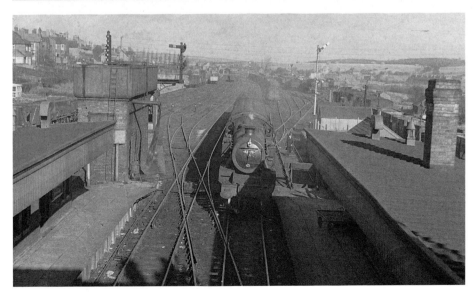

Hednesford Station

Lower left: William Stanier designed 2-cylinder 2-6-4T No 42579, built by the North British Locomotive Company in Glasgow in 1936 and withdrawn in June 1962, runs in with a Rugeley Trent Valley to Walsall local passenger. The station was demolished after the passenger service was withdrawn in January 1965 and the sidings were removed following the closure of all local collieries in the 1970s. The signal box (formerly No 1), seen behind the water tower, remains in operation. No 2 Signal Box closed on 14th January 1973 and No 3 from 18th December 1977. Passenger services were reinstated from Walsall to Hednesford in 1989, using newly erected platforms. It is hoped that one day funding will be made available to extend this service to Rugeley and Stafford. *29th October 1952*

Annesley Motive Power Depot (38B)

Top right: This H A Ivatt designed 4-4-2T was built for the Great Northern Railway between 1898 and 1907 and was later one of the LNER C12 class. Over 30 were still in service in 1953, including this one, 67363. *15th March 1953*

Rugby Central

Centre right: LNER A3 class 4-6-2 No 60059 *Tracery* enters the station with the 11.56 up departure for Marylebone. The signal gantry is of interest. Each arm has a white painted backing board to assist approaching drivers to identify the arm's position in the day time against the overbridge wall. The gantry also displays a 'D' symbol which informs drivers brought to a stand there, that the signals are not protected by track circuits, and as there is no telephone here his fireman must be sent to inform the signalman of the train's position by pressing the plunger situated at the base of the signal post. The locomotive was built at Doncaster in February 1925 as LNER No 2558 and was withdrawn in December 1962. *28th March 1953*

Lichfield Trent Valley Station

Below: The 15.45 London Euston to Manchester London Road express is hauled by a Longsight 'Jubilee' class 4-6-0, No 45555 *Quebec*. The 'Jubilee' is in the hands of Driver Munslow from Camden Shed's top link. This locomotive was built at Crewe works in June 1934 and withdrawn from service in August 1963. It retains the small Fowler 3500 gallon tender at this date. *22nd April 1953*

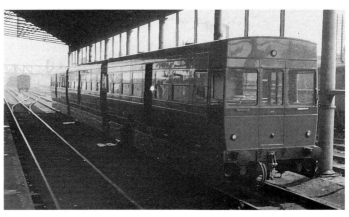

Lichfield Trent Valley

Above: 'Patriot' class 4-6-0 No 45535 *Sir Herbert Walker, K.C.B.* works north with the 12.55 London Euston to Blackpool Central. This was another rebuild of a LNWR 'Claughton'. When it emerged from Derby Works in 1933 it was numbered 5997. Under the LMS renumbering of 1934 it became No 5535. Naming took place in 1937 and the Stanier rebuilding with a 2A taper boiler, new cylinders and double chimney took place at Crewe Works in 1948. It was withdrawn from service in 1963. *3rd April 1953*

Rugby Midland Station

Above: An experiment with 4-wheeled railbuses, made up into a 3-car set, was initiated in 1952 by ACV Sales Limited. This was an enterprising effort, allegedly spoilt by poor riding qualities. The end cars were powered by 6-cylinder diesel engines, the centre one was unpowered. A cross between a multiple-unit and a railcar, externally it was finished in an attractive grey livery with a red band; internally it was more like a road bus. The set was on its way to North Wales for trials on some branch lines there. *21st May 1953*

Rugby Midland

Left: 'Jubilee' class 4-6-0 No 45688 *Polyphemus*, coasts over the permanent up through speed restriction with the 11.55 Wolverhampton High Level to London Euston express. Note the Coronation crown headboard which many London Midland Region expresses carried over the two week period around the date of the Coronation in June 1953. *6th June 1953*

Below: Stanier Class 8F 2-8-0 No 48603, built at Eastleigh works in 1943, pulls away up the Northampton line with the 08.30 Charnwood to Willesden goods. It is interesting to note that the up fast, to the left of the train, is made up of lengths of 60ft bullhead rail, not yet superceded by flat bottomed rail. *21st May 1953*

Lichfield Trent Valley High Level

Above: The 09.17 Wolverhampton High Level to Burton-on-Trent local passenger is headed by former Midland Railway 4-4-0 No 40364, which was built at Derby in 1886 and subsequently rebuilt by Deeley and Fowler. *9th June 1953*

Lichfield Trent Valley

Below: WD 2-8-0 No 90707 carries a Mirfield (25D) shed plate. It was built by the Vulcan Foundry in February 1945 as No 79268 and sent to Europe. Repatriated from Belgium in 1947 it was stored at Swindon before being taken into BR ownership in Decem- ber 1948. No 90707 is seen here working the 08.04 Crewe to Whitemoor goods, awaiting a path off the up slow over the two-track section to Tamworth. On the left of the picture is the original station opened in December 1847 and closed in July 1871 when a new station on the current site was opened. *11th June 1953*

Rugby Midland

Above: Rebuilt ex-LMS 'Jubilee' class 4-6-0 No 45736 *Phoenix*, with the 09.10 Llandudno to London Euston, takes the Northampton line under the GCR 'birdcage' bridge. No 45736 was built at Crewe in November 1936 and rebuilt with a 2A taper boiler in April 1942, the power classification being increased from 5XP to 6P and in 1951 to 7P. Only one other 'Jubilee,' No 45735 *Comet*, was similarly rebuilt. *28th July 1953*

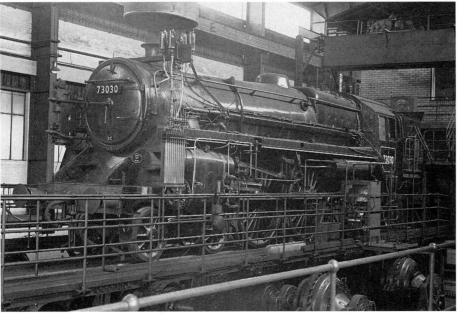

Rugby Locomotive Testing Station

Centre left: Fitted up and ready for testing BR Standard Class 5 4-6-0 No 73030, built at Derby the previous month, rests on the rollers on its first day at the station, a joint LMS/LNER project started in 1937 but not commissioned until October 1948. The last testing was carried out in 1965, the machinery was dismantled in 1970 and the building demolished in 1984. No 73030 was withdrawn in August 1965 . *23rd July 1953*

Lichfield Trent Valley High Level

Left: Walsall (3C) allocated, Fowler-designed 0-6-0 4F No 44078 heads a bank holiday half-day excursion, from Wolverhampton High Level to Alton Towers. This locomotive, built in 1925, was one of 575 members of this class constructed between 1924 and 1941. The Midland machines were mainly right-hand drive while those built by the LMS were left-hand drive. The line over which this train would have run was closed between Uttoxeter and Alton Towers in 1965 and between Burton and Tutbury in 1968. *2nd August 1953*

Lichfield Trent Valley High Level

Above: The 09.17 Wolverhampton High Level to Burton-on-Trent local passenger service headed by LMS Class 2P 4-4-0 No 40436, allocated to Burton (17B) MPD, coasts towards the station. The Wolverhampton, Walsall, Lichfield and Burton local service ceased in January 1965. *3rd August 1953*

116 mp West Coast Main Line

Centre right: BR Standard 'Britannia' Class 7MT 4-6-2 No 70043 leaves Lichfield Trent Valley with the 08.20 Manchester London Road to London Euston. Built at Crewe Works in June 1953, it was fitted with two Westinghouse air brake pumps for working heavy freight trains and was eventually allocated to Longsight (9A) MPD, with the similarly equipped No 70044. The pumps were later removed, the smoke deflectors carried by the rest of the class fitted, and 70043 was named *Earl Kitchener*. It was withdrawn from Crewe South (5B) MPD in August 1965. *3rd August 1953*

Rugby Midland

Right: An extra cattle train from Holyhead to Maiden Lane, displaying most of its reporting number FW545, (FW = Freight, Western Division) takes the up main line headed by ex-LMS 'Patriot' class 4-6-0 No 45516 *The Bedfordshire & Hertfordshire Regiment.* Originally LNWR 'Claughton' No 103, then LMS No 5982 and post-1934 No 5516, she was withdrawn in '61. Maiden Lane, reached from Willesden via the North London Line, was the destination for most of the cattle traffic brought in from Ireland through Holyhead. *12th September 1953*

Left: Former LMSR 3-cylinder Compound 4-4-0 No 41163, built by the Vulcan Foundry in 1925 and 'Jubilee' class 4-6-0 No 45741 *Leinster*, double-head the 11.55 Wolverhampton High Level to London Euston on the up through line. This train was normally handled throughout by a Bushbury (3B) MPD-allocated 'Jubilee' but was usually strengthened on Fridays. The high LNWR gantry above the first and second coaches controlled trains coming off the Midland line from Wigston, which opened in 1840 and closed in 1969. Rugby No 5 Signal Box can also be seen over the fourth and fifth coaches. *18th September 1953*

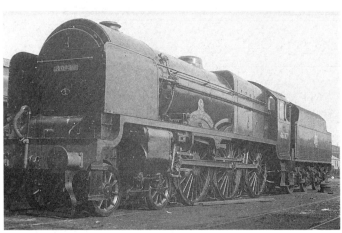

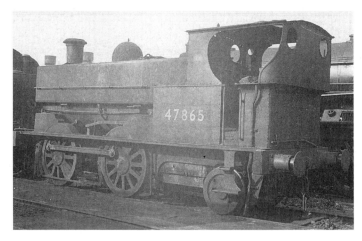

Crewe Works

Above: The last parallel-boilered 'Royal Scot' class 4-6-0 goes through the Works, even though conversion to a 2A taper boiler was only two years away. No 46137 *The Prince of Wales's Volunteers (South Lancashire)* was built by the North British Locomotive Company in 1927. Originally named *Vesta*, No 46137 was withdrawn by BR in October 1962. *27th September 1953*

Above right: This is one of two LNWR 0-4-2 pannier tanks designed by F C Webb, introduced in 1896 and known as 'bissells' after the under-cab trailing truck. They came into BR stock and were employed as works shunters. Here No 47865, the former LNWR No 3529 which became LMSR No 6415 in 1927 and No 7865 in 1934, rests in the works yard. *27th September 1953*

Below left: Lancashire & Yorkshire Railway

0-6-0 No 1030, one of 448 introduced by J A Aspinall, as the F19 class, and built between 1889 and 1917. Renumbered by the LMSR as No 12093 and subsequently 52093 in BR stock, some members of the class were later rebuilt with a Belpaire firebox and an extended smokebox but No 52093 is in pretty much original condition. Although the locomotive is carrying a Wigan (27D) MPD allocation plate, it was in use as a works shunter. *27th September 1953*

Opposite page, top: Class 5MT No 44738, built at Crewe, was one of the 22 'Black 5s' constructed between 1948 and 1951 to Stanier's design, but fitted with Caprotti valve gear. Tests are in progress here and an 'indicator' shelter has been provided to protect, from the elements, the technical staff recording data while travelling on the front of the engine. *27th September 1953*

Opposite page, bottom: A BR Standard Class 2MT 2-6-2T No 84017, under construction. It was scrapped only 13 years later by Arnott Young of Parkgate after withdrawal in January 1966. The class totalled 30, Nos 84000 to 840019 being built at Crewe and Nos 84020 to 84029 at Darlington works. Designed at Derby the 84000 locomotives were a tank engine version of the 78000 2-6-0s which in turn were derived from Ivatt's 1946 design for the LMSR numbered in the sequence 46400 to 46527. *27th September 1953*

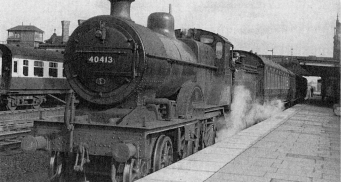

Scalford Station – GN & LNW Joint

Above: The 10.47 all-stations local from Nottingham Victoria to Northampton Castle pauses at Scalford, one week before the line closed. Working the train is 2P 4-4-0 No 40464 from Northampton (2E) MPD. This locomotive was built at Derby in 1895 and was rebuilt twice in its lifetime. *28th November 1953*

Tamworth Low Level Station

Above: Ex-Midland Railway 4-4-0 class 2P No 40413, allocated to Crewe North (5A) MPD, and originally built at Derby in the early 1890s, waits with the 13.10 Nuneaton Trent Valley to Stafford local. To the left of the picture can be seen the signal box at the Derby end of the up platform of Tamworth High Level Station. This signal box was demolished following the introduction of Multiple Aspect Signalling, which was controlled from Saltley PSB, in August 1969. 27th *February 1954*

Rugby Midland

Left: 'The Merseyside Express', the 10.10 Liverpool Lime Street to London Euston opens up while moving off the permanent speed restriction from the up through to up fast, headed by LMSR 'Princess Royal' class 4-6-2 No 46208 *Princess Helena Victoria*, built at Crewe in August 1935 and withdrawn from service in October 1962. No 1 Signal Box is seen to the left and the shed yard (2A) beyond the train. *27th February 1954*

Rugby Midland Station

Above: A trade visit to Cadbury's factory at Bournville, in Birmingham, brings a train of Southern Region stock, on a working which had originated in Portsmouth, through Rugby Station. Headed by LMSR class 5MT 4-6-0 No 44875, the train is passing No 4 Signal Box on the down through line. This box closed in September 1964 when the Rugby PSB opened. Overhead line equipment was switched on between Kilsby Tunnel North Ground Frame (79 mile post) and Nuneaton Trent Valley (96½ mile post), in the same period. *8th April 1954*

Rugby, Clifton Road – 81½ mp WCML

Right: LMSR 'Compound' 4-4-0 No 40933 pilots 'Jubilee' 4-6-0 No 45703 *Thunderer* on the 11.55 Wolverhampton High Level to London Euston. This train ran under 'XL Limit' timings, with a maximum load of 350 tons for a class 6P locomotive between Birmingham and London. When strengthening was required, usually on Fridays, a pilot was attached at Birmingham, normally a Monument Lane (3E) Compound. No 40933, seen here, is attached to a non-standard tender which resembles a Fowler 3500 gallon narrow tender with the coal rails removed and a curved top sheeting welded in its place. *9th April 1954*

Buildwas Station

Right: Former GWR Churchward Mogul No 6359, then allocated to Worcester (85A) shed, with a freight for the Severn Valley Line. One of only two survivors of this class, No 7325, can still be seen at work on the preserved part of the SVR between Bridgnorth and Kidderminster. *1st May 1954*

Kidderminster Station

Below: Former GWR 2-6-2T No 4596, allocated to Kidderminster (85D) MPD has arrived with the 15.50 local passenger train from Shrewsbury via the Severn Valley line and run round its train. In the up platform stands ex-GWR diesel railcar No 19, a 48 seat vehicle with a 210 bhp engine, built in 1940 at Swindon, working the 17.48 service to Bewdley. The original station was demolished in 1968, replaced by a much more austere modern building. *1st May 1954*

Wellington Station, Salop

Left: Former GWR 5700 class 0-6-0PT No 3613, allocated to Wellington (84H) MPD, stands with the 15.10 local passenger to Much Wenlock in the down bay platform. The Much Wenlock service ceased in 1962. *1st May 1954*

Rugby Midland

Centre left: Bound for the International Railway Congress exhibition in London, is the 'Fell' diesel mechanical locomotive No 10100, designed by H G Ivatt, and built at Derby works in 1951. Its eight 4ft 3in diameter driving wheels were originally coupled together to give a 4-8-4 wheel arrangement, but in 1954 these were split into the 4-4-4-4 system as seen here. Its short career ended following a fire at Manchester Central in 1958. Withdrawn in November 1960, it was cut up at Derby works in January 1962. *17th May 1954*

Rugby, Clifton Road

Below: Former LMSR 2-8-0 No 48108 proceeds along the up goods line to Hillmorton with three exhibits for the International Railway Congress exhibition in London The 'Fell' is leading, followed by BR class 5MT 4-6-0 No 73050, just recently built at Derby (and eventually withdrawn in June 1968 to be preserved on the Nene Valley Railway as *City of Peterborough*) and diesel electric 350hp shunter No 3046, later 08 033, also newly constructed at Derby. The train was routed via Leicester, Wigston, Rugby and Northampton. *17th May 1954*

Rugby Midland

Right: Former LMSR 2-8-0 No 48633, built at Brighton in 1943 and allocated to Willesden (1A) MPD , tows 1500V DC Co-Co electric No 27002, built at Gorton in May 1954 (works No 1067) for the Manchester to Sheffield electrification. Named *Aurora* in June 1959, No 27002 was withdrawn from service in September 1968 and sold to the Netherlands State Railway the following year. *18th May 1954*

Rugby Midland

Above: Former LMSR 'Jubilee' class 4-6-0 No 45688 *Polyphemus*, takes the 11.55 Wolverhampton High Level to London Euston under the 'birdcage' bridge while coasting over the PSR (permanent speed restriction) from up through to up fast lines. Rugby No 1 Signal Box, opened in 1884, is to the left, and the coaling plant of Rugby MPD (2A) is to the right. *27th July 1954*

Hademore Crossing – 114 mp WCML

Right: BR Standard 8P Caprotti 4-6-2 No 71000 *Duke of Gloucester* passes over the down line trough with 'The Mid-day Scot', the 13.15 London Euston to Glasgow Central. Adverse signals approaching Hademore Signal Box has forced the driver to apply the sanders in a vain attempt to reach sufficient speed to gather water – otherwise an enforced stop will have to be made before reaching the next troughs at Whitmore, 34 miles north. *31st July 1954*

Bromshall Junction

Above: LMSR Horwich 'Crab' 2-6-0 No 42938, built at Crewe works in 1932, comes through the clipped up junction of the former GNR Uttoxeter to Stafford line, closed in 1951 and lifted in the 1960s, with the 11.20 Crewe - Derby local stopping train. *14th September 1954*

Bromshall Tunnel

Far left: The Great Northern Railway branch from Uttoxeter to Stafford, which opened in 1867 and finally closed in 1951, had one tunnel of 321 yards length, viewed here at the west portal. The Stephenson Locomotive Society special, a 3-coach push-pull set, hauled by Ivatt 2-6-2T No 41224, had to cope with these encroaching jungle conditions when it operated the last passenger train on the line on 23rd March 1957. *14th August 1954*

Grindley Station

Centre left: Closed to passengers in 1939, this view shows the staggered platforms. The loop line is the right-hand one and the signal box still has its name board attached. The waiting shelter in the foreground was dismantled and re-erected in the Engineer's yard at Walsall. *14th August 1954*

Marshall's Siding – 108 mp WCML

Bottom: Former LMSR 'Jubilee' class 4-6-0 No 45634 *Trinidad* on the up fast with the 08.35 Sundays only Liverpool Lime Street to London Euston. The loop next to the down slow line was opened in 1890 to help take away the coal produced from several pits in the vicinity. Tracks between Tamworth and Atherstone were quadrupled in July 1901. Marshall's was closed in 1961 and Amington Signal Box, the next one north, closed in November 1962 with the introduction of multiple aspect signalling between Ashby Junction and Lichfield Trent Valley. The overhead line equipment was switched on between Lichfield Trent Valley and Nuneaton Trent Valley in January 1964. *12th September 1954*

Lichfield Trent Valley High Level

Right: Taking water from the parachute column while working the 10.32 Burton-on-Trent to Birmingham New Street local passenger train, is former LMSR 2-6-4T No 42421, built at Derby works in 1934 and withdrawn in August 1964. The locomotive carries a 3E Monument Lane Motive Power Depot, shed plate. *5th February 1955*

Etwall Signal Box

Below: The Great Northern Railway's line from Derby Friargate to Egginton Junction opened to passengers in 1878 and closed in 1939, but was retained for specials and freight. The section between Egginton Junction and Mickleover now forms the Derby Technical Centre's test track. *12th January 1955*

Lichfield City Station

Below: The 08.00 semi-fast service to Birmingham New Street, which omitted stops between Wylde Green and Vauxhall, is about to leave behind BR class 2MT 2-6-0 No 78038, allocated to Bescot (3A) MPD. Built in November 1954, one of the class of 65, all constructed at Darlington between 1952 and 1956, 78038 was withdrawn from service in August 1966. DMUs took this service over on 5th March 1956. *2nd April 1955*

Birmingham New Street Station

Above: No 10800 was a 827hp Bo-Bo diesel built by the North British Locomotive Company in conjunction with the BTH Company, in 1950. Withdrawn in 1958 and stored at Doncaster Works, it was sold to Brush Limited at Loughborough in 1962, who modified it for further tests. It is seen here moving the empty stock of the 06.35 ex-Yarmouth Vauxhall to Monument Lane carriage shed, for servicing. *2nd April 1955*

Colwich Junction

Above: Southern Railway designed 1 Co-Co 1 1760 hp diesel electric No 10201, built at Ashford works in 1950, with No 1 end leading, heads the 12.00 London Euston to Crewe near the end of the four track section. The brick works with its siding to the left of the train have long since gone. This early diesel electric was withdrawn in 1963. *26th April 1955*

Armitage – 121½ mp WCML

Centre left: Rebuilt LMSR 'Royal Scot' class 4-6-0 No 46147 *The Northamptonshire Regiment* heads the 08.00 Blackpool Central to London Euston on the up fast towards the end of the four-track section. The down slow (extreme left) was transposed with the down fast (second left) in December 1961 to enable trains bound for the Stoke line from Colwich Junction to take the slow line and avoid delay to following WCML trains travelling via Stafford. The former were often slowed or stopped by conflicting up train movements over the junction at Colwich. *9th April 1955*

Armitage – 121½ mp WCML

Centre right: 'The Merseyside Express' behind ex-LMSR 4-6-2 No 46200 *Princess Royal*, built at Crewe in July 1933, and withdrawn November 1962. *9th April 1955*

Armitage Station – 121 mp WCML

Above: Beames LNWR 0-8-0 No 2178 of the G2 class, built at Crewe and converted from the original Compound design in 1922. Now BR No 49454 with tender cab, it passes with an up hopper train from Simonswood to Greys. The station closed 11th June 1960. *7th December 1955*

Kingsbury Station

Centre right: Westminster Bank Railway Society railtour from Paddington to Derby Works formed of GWR railcars Nos 33 and 38, with TO W1096 in the middle. Built in 1942 at Swindon Works, in conjuction with AEC, these railcars had four engines giving a total of 420 bhp. The station, between Tamworth and Water Orton, closed in March 1968; the buildings were demolished in 1970 and the platforms were removed the following year. *2nd October 1955*

Wolverhampton Works

Bottom right: Seen here receiving attention are 5700 class 0-6-0PT No 9635; 2251 class 0-6-0 No 3211 – allocated to Didcot (81E), and 'Hall' 4-6-0 No 6941 *Fillongley Hall.* Opened by the Shrewsbury & Birmingham Railway in 1849 and absorbed into the GWR in 1854, Wolverhampton produced its first locomotive in 1859, a Joseph Armstrong-designed 2-2-2. All new construction was transferred to Swindon in 1908. The last newly built engine was a 2-6-2T, No 4519 and the last repair was carried out in February 1964 to 2-8-0 No 2859. Final closure came in June 1964. *18th February 1956*

Birmingham New Street Station

Left: The 'Pines Express' leaves the west end of No 9 platform for Bournemouth, via Mangotsfield, Bath and the Somerset & Dorset line, banked by former Midland Railway 483 class 4-4-0 No 40511, built at Derby in 1898 and allocated to Saltley (21A) MPD at this time. The Midland side shunting engine at New Street Station was frequently called upon to bank the heavier expresses as far as Church Road Junction, dropping back through the crossover on to the up line to return to New Street. *18th February 1956*

Hasland Motive Power Depot (18C)

Centre left: Stabled in the roofless roundhouse are Stanier 2-8-0 No 48075, built by Vulcan Foundry at Newton-le-Willows in 1936, and S W Johnson's Midland Railway class 2P 4-4-0 No 40337, built at Derby in 1882. Both locomotives carry Hasland shed plates. The Hasland shed code was changed to 16H in 1963, just a year before it closed. *11th March 1956*

Below: A pair of Garratts are seen on shed, with No 47971 in the foreground. The LMSR initially purchased three Garratt 2-6-0+0-6-2 locomotives from Beyer Peacock in 1927, and these were numbered 4997 to 4999. A further 30 were supplied in 1930, taking the numbers 4967 to 4996. Water capacity in the leading tank was 3030 gallons whilst the rear tank/bunker carried 1470 gallons and 9 tons of coal. Most were eventually fitted with rotary bunkers. Renumbering took place in 1938-9 to Nos 7967-7999, with the prefix '4' being added under the BR (LM Region) scheme. Withdrawals started in June 1953 and were completed, with 47994 being the last to go, in April 1958. *11th March 1956*

Canklow Motive Power Depot (19C)

Above: Two of S W Johnson's numerous former Midland Railway 2F 0-6-0s, Nos 58238 and 58198, are nearest the camera. First introduced in 1875 with a round top firebox, later batches and rebuilds of the earlier locomotives had Belpaire fireboxes. In 1957, 79 of these machines were still in service with BR. This depot, situated near Rotherham, was transferred to the Eastern Region in 1958 and allocated the shed code 41D. It closed in 1965. *11th March 1956*

Crewe Works

Centre right: BR Standard class 9F 2-10-0 No 92081, seen here under construction, was one of 39 of this class built at Crewe in that year. This particular locomotive was withdrawn in February 1966 after a working life of less than 10 years. *8th April 1956*

Lickey Incline – Blackwell

Right: The fireman takes a welcome drink from his billycan while descending down to Bromsgrove aboard the Midland Railway's unique Fowler-designed 0-10-0, No 58100 (nicknamed 'Big Bertha'), in company with 0-6-0T No 47565. The 0-10-0 was built at Derby in 1919, with four 16¾in x 28in cylinders, inclined at 1 in 7, all driving on to the centre pair of 4ft 7½in driving wheels. In 1922 it was fitted with a headlight in front of the chimney, powered by a generator under the cab. Originally numbered 2290, it was renumbered 22290 in October 1947 and 58100 in January 1949. Its last banking duties on the 1 in 37½ incline came two days after this picture was taken. The engine was moved to Derby and cut up in April 1957. *4th May 1956*

Hugglescote Station

Above: The L&NW and MR joint line from Nuneaton to Moira opened in August 1873 and the branch from Shackerstone Junction to Coalville and Loughborough Derby Road in April 1883. Passenger services on both lines ceased in April 1931 followed by complete closure in 1971. However, the section from Shackerstone Junction to Market Bosworth and Shenton has been preserved. This scene shows a Bowen Cooke LNWR G1 class 0-8-0 No 49342 (LNW No 2568) stopped with a Banbury bound coal train, to pick up water churns outside the Midland Railway designed signal box. *20th June 1956*

Heather & Ibstock

Above: Although closed to passengers in April 1931, the platforms and the MR-type signal box were still in situ in 1956. Note the very elaborate track layout for such a small station. This scene has long disappeared. *20th June 1956*

Castle Ashby & Earls Barton Station

Centre left: The 15.42 Wellingborough London Road to Northampton Castle 'push-pull motor' service propelled by ex-LMS Ivatt 2-6-2T 41328 passes ex-LMS 4F 0-6-0 44563, a Rose Grove (24B) allocated locomotive, fitted with the Automatic Warning System apparatus, standing in the siding with the local pick-up goods to Northampton Bridge Street. Opened by the London & Birmingham Railway in June 1845, the line closed to passenger services in May 1964 and freight in August 1966. *27th June 1956*

Carwardine Signal Box – 122¾mp WCML

Bottom left: Carwardine Signal Box, located approximately 1 mile from the nearest road access, and controlling just home and distant signals on each of the four tracks, was purely a block post and was often switched out, as was the case on this occasion, due to the shortage of signalmen. At busy times, it provided an additional block section between Armitage (1m 861 yds south) and Rugeley No 1 (1m 685yds north). Closure came in 1957-8 when colour light intermediate block signals were installed. Multiple aspect signalling was introduced between Colwich Junction and Lichfield Trent Valley in July 1962, this area being controlled first from Rugeley No 1 and later by Colwich Junction. Overhead line equipment was energised in August 1963 between Stafford and Lichfield Trent Valley. Former LMS rebuilt 'Royal Scot' class 4-6-0 No 46131 *The Royal Warwickshire Regiment*, is seen here working the 12.37(SO) London Euston to Manchester London Road. *21st July 1956*

Shackerstone Junction

Above: Ex-LMSR Stanier 2-8-0 No 48401, built at Swindon works in 1943, approaches the former station and junction with the 10.40 Nuneaton to Burton freight. The Midland Railway Society, now known as the Shackerstone Railway Society, moved into the station in 1970 when restoration of the 4¼ miles of single line to Shenton, now marketed as 'The Battlefield Line', was begun. *27th July 1956*

Shackerstone Junction Signal Box

Below: The double track up from Nuneaton splits into two single lines – left to Moira and right to Coalville and Loughborough Derby Road. Part of the line was used to store wagons before the final closure at the beginning of the 1970s. *27th July 1956*

Clifton Station

Left: This North Staffordshire Railway station, on the Uttoxeter to Ashbourne line, opened in 1852 and closed in October 1954. *12th August 1956*

Nailsworth Yard

Centre left: S W Johnson-designed former Midland Railway 0-6-0T No 41748 takes water at the end of the branch from Stonehouse on the Gloucester to Bristol line. The open cab afforded no weather protection when running bunker first. *7th September 1956*

Derby Works

Centre right: Ex-works engineer's department 0-4-0DM locomotive ED7, built in 1940 by J Fowler & Co of Leeds as No 22891, was eventually to be withdrawn from service in February 1964. *21st October 1956*

Shenstone

Above: Derby-built DMU twin-set Nos 79129 and 79650, cross what was the A38 (now the A5127) with the 11.03 Sundays only Lichfield City to Birmingham New Street service. DMUs replaced steam in 1956; but these were in turn made redundant in November 1992 following electrification and the start of electric services between Lichfield Trent Valley High Level and Birmingham New Street. A further development occurred when the first of the new Class 323 EMUs worked through from Lichfield to Redditch on 7th February 1994. *20th January 1957*

West Coast Main Line – 117 mp

Right: The prototype 3300hp English Electric Co-Co locomotive *Deltic* was built in 1955, and is seen here heading the 13.35 London Euston to Blackpool Central whilst on trials with BR. Withdrawn in 1960, it was presented to the Science Museum in 1963 and in 1993 it moved to the National Railway Museum in York. Twenty-two 'Deltics' were later acquired by BR for use on the ECML. *16th February 1957*

Crewe Works

Centre left: Probably the last working LNWR 'Cauliflower' 0-6-0, LNW No 314 became LMS 8427 and later 28427, ending up as BR No 58427. Carrying a 8D (Widnes) shed plate, it was retained at Crewe works for possible preservation for over 12 months, but sadly was eventually scrapped. *17th February 1957*

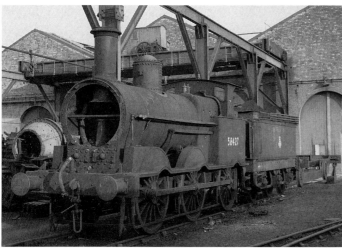

Crewe Works

Centre right: With the scrapping of all the former LNWR works shunters, other former LMS constituent companies' locomotives were drafted in. One of these was an ex-Caledonian Railway 0-4-0 saddle tank, built as No 612 at St Rollox works in Glasgow in 1895: an example of a class of 39 locomotives constructed between 1878 and 1908. It was renumbered 16027 by the LMS and 56027 by BR. *17th February 1957*

Great Bridge

Right: W G Bagnall Ltd of Stafford built this 0-4-0ST, works No 2450, named *J.T. Daly,* in 1931. Owned by Horseley Bridge & Thomas Piggott Limited, the locomotive shunted at their site, which adjoined the former South Staffordshire Railway line between Dudley Port Low Level and Great Bridge. The locomotive was for a time resident at Alderney in the Channel Islands. *2nd March 1957*

Birmingham Snow Hill Station

Left: It was the exception to witness a passenger train passing through non-stop. Here, ex-GWR 'Modified Hall' class 4-6-0 No 7902 *Eaton Mascot Hall*, built at Swindon in March 1949 and withdrawn in June 1964, works on the down through line with the 10.35 football special from Paddington to The Hawthorns Halt, for the West Bromwich Albion ground. *2nd February 1957*

Coventry Motive Power Depot (2D)

Centre left: The shed was situated in the angle between the Rugby and Leamington lines, now occupied by the Coventry Power Signal Box. The roof was renewed in 1957 and the structure partially rebuilt in 1958, only for the depot to be closed with the introduction of DMUs in 1959. In 1950 the shed code was changed from 2F to 2D. Outside are Stanier 2-6-4T No 42489 and 2-6-2T No 40138, which were built respectively at Derby in 1937 and 1935 and withdrawn in 1964 and 1962. *21st March 1957*

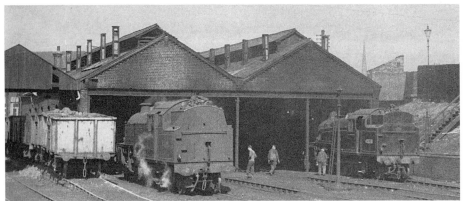

Hilton Main Colliery, Featherstone

Bottom: Working from the loco shed at the site of Hollybank Colliery, Essington, Hunslet Engine Company 0-6-0ST of 1936 (works No 1821), *Carol Ann No 5*, shunts in harness with No 2, a Hudswell Clarke 0-6-0ST of 1943 (works No 1752, ex-WD 75091). The latter took part in the 'Rocket 150' celebrations at Rainhill in 1980 and is now preserved at The Railway Age at Crewe with the name *Robert*. *30th March 1957*

Welshpool Station

Right: GWR 'Manor' class 4-6-0 No 7802 *Bradley Manor* stands in the bay platform with the 12.25 local passenger to Oswestry. The line from Buttington Junction to Oswestry used by this service closed on 18th January 1965. This locomotive, which was built at Swindon Works in January 1938 and withdrawn in November 1965, is now preserved on the Severn Valley Railway. Originally purchased as a source of spare parts for sister locomotive No 7812 *Erlestoke Manor*, No 7802 was back in steam in 1994 and was used on main line specials in the West Country in 1995.
13th April 1957

Coalville Town Station

Above: The Railway Enthusiasts' Club 'Charnwood Forester' special from London, drawn here by former Midland Railway class 3F 0-6-0 No 43728, is en route, via Coalville Junction and (propel to) Charnwood Forest Junction to Loughborough Derby Road. Coalville shed to the left of the picture had its 15D code changed to 15E in 1963, just two years before it closed.
14th April 1957

Calverton Colliery Signal Box

Right: Organised by the Stephenson Locomotive Society, this 'Nottinghamshire Coalfields' special was worked by BR Standard 2-6-2T No 84006, allocated to Burton (17B) MPD, hauling a 3-coach push-pull set. *27th April 1957*

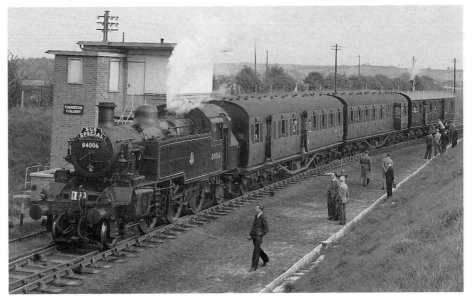

Ashchurch Station

Above: The double tracks in the foreground are those of the main Bristol to Birmingham route, which are crossed on the level here by the single line branch which ran from Upton upon Severn to Barnt Green through Evesham and Redditch. This view, looking east, shows Ashchurch Level Crossing signal box with the single track level crossing still in use. The latter was taken out of use in May 1957 and the signal box closed with the opening of a new box on the down side, west of the station, in July 1958. This new box was itself closed within 5 years due to the opening of the Gloucester Power Box. Ashchurch Station was closed in November 1971 but the local Council has plans for a 'Park and Ride' station on the site in the future. *28th April 1957*

Lichfield Trent Valley

Left: Stanier-designed class 5MT 2-6-0 No 42948, built at Crewe works in 1933, gets under way with the evening pick-up freight from Tamworth to Harlescott, near Shrewsbury. The pick-up freight, once an everyday sight on the railways of Britain, has now been consigned to the pages of railway history, apart from the occasional re-enactment on preserved lines. The only survivor of the class, No 42968, can on occasions be seen hauling one of these on the Severn Valley Railway. *11th May 1957*

Lichfield Trent Valley – 117 mp

Above: Former LMSR 'Royal Scot' class 4-6-0 No 46122 *Royal Ulster Rifleman,* working the 15.45 London Euston to Manchester London Road service. *1st July 1957*

Shrewsbury Station

Centre right: A Paddington-bound express stands waiting to leave at the south end of the station headed by ex-GWR 'County' class 4-6-0 No 1008 *County of Cardigan,* built at Swindon in December 1945, withdrawn in October 1963 and scrapped by Cashmores at Newport. *18th May 1957*

Lichfield Trent Valley – 117 mp

Right: Here, making smoke by request, the 16.35 Coventry to Stafford local, headed by LMSR 2P No 40678, built at Derby works in 1932 and allocated to Stafford (5C) depot, gets away after making the connection out of the 15.45 London Euston to Manchester London Road, routed over the North Staffs line from Colwich Junction. The local was booked to arrive at Lichfield at 17.56 where all passengers were detrained and the empty coaching stock would draw forward towards No 2 Signal Box, clear of the down-slow to fast crossover. After the express' departure at 18.11 the stock set back into the platform, loaded up and departed, all stations to Stafford at 18.20. *1st July 1957*

Vauxhall Station

Above: 'Battle of Britain' class No 34053 *Sir Keith Park* gets under way from London Waterloo Station with a south coast express. No 34053 has been preserved. *7th July 1957*

Hatton Bank

Below: The 08.55 Margate to Birmingham Snow Hill, composed of ex-LMSR opens, a Gresley Brake and seven Southern vehicles, tackles the 1 in 100 gradient on the GWR route from London to Birmingham between Warwick and Lapworth, headed by ex-GWR 4300 class 2-6-0 No 6379. The circular patch on the smokebox side suggests the boiler has previously been fitted to a locomotive with outside steam pipes. *20th July 1957*

Tenbury Wells Station

Above: The Stephenson Locomotive Society organised a trip to mark the centenary of the Leominster to Kington branch. The special consisted of two auto-trailers worked by GWR 1400 class 0-4-2T No 1455, allocated to Hereford (85C) MPD. *27th July 1957*

Peascliff Tunnel – 108 mp East Coast Main Line

Below: LNER A1 class 4-6-2 No 60157 *Great Eastern*, emerges from the 967 yard tunnel with an up-express. Built at Doncaster in November 1949, this Pacific was withdrawn in January 1965 and scrapped by Drapers of Hull in March 1965. *17th August 1957*

Peascliff Tunnel – 108 mp ECML

Left: Streamlined ex-LNER A4 4-6-2 Pacific No 60012 *Commonwealth of Australia*, was built at Doncaster in June 1937 and withdrawn in August 1964. It is seen here working an up express. Although 'The Elizabethan' headboard is displayed, this is not in fact that famous train, as the photograph was taken on a Saturday and 'The Elizabethan' only ran Mondays to Fridays! Normally the fireman would reverse the board when placing the head-lamps over the buffers. *17th August 1957*

Centre left: Ex-LNER 3-cylinder V2 class 2-6-2 No 60829 was built at Doncaster Works in 1938. This locomotive is fitted with the original smaller outside steam pipes and is working a Kings Cross to Newcastle express. Peascliffe Tunnel is between Barkston Junction and Grantham. *17th August 1957*

Ryde St Johns Road Station, IoW

Below: Class O2 0-4-4T No W27 *Merstone* with a stopping train from Ryde Pierhead to Ventnor. During the summer timetable the section to Smallbrook Junction was worked as a normal double track section. In the winter months Smallbrook Junction was closed and trains departed for Ventnor or Cowes lines from St Johns over the two adjacent but separate single lines. At these times the missing arms were reinstated on the signal gantry illustrated. *17th August 1957*

Broxton Station

Above: The 14.12 (SO) Chester General to Whitchurch local passenger service worked by ex-LMS class 2P 4-4-0 No 40660, built at Crewe works in 1931, pauses beside the attractive signal box. The 14 mile branch, running from Tattenhall Junction on the Crewe to Chester line, opened in 1872 and closed to passengers on 14th September 1957. Freight services lasted until 1963. Note the LNW lower quadrant home signal and trespass notice. *7th September 1957*

Rawnsley Locomotive Shed (NCB)

Opposite page: The former Cannock & Rugeley Colliery Company kept up to eight locomotives, many of them vintage machines, in this straight roaded shed off the Cannock Wood to Chase Terrace road, to work on the BR single track branch to Hednesford No 1 SB and on the Cross Keys to Littleton Junction line. *Centre right:* No 5 *Beaudesert*, was a Fox Walker & Co 0-6-0ST, works No 266, built in 1875; *Bottom:* 0-6-0T No 9 *Cannock Wood* was a Stroudley class E1 built at Brighton works in 1877 for the London, Brighton & South Coast Railway as 110 *Burgundy*. It was withdrawn from service in February 1927 and sold to the colliery in April of that year for £925. Following withdrawal by the NCB in 1963, it was sold to the Railway Preservation Society in 1964 for £240 and kept at their Hednesford site until the lease expired, at which time it moved to the East Somerset Railway at Cranmore where full restoration was undertaken and the locomotive steamed. *14th December 1957*

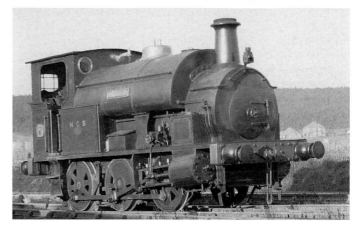

Grove Colliery, Little Wyrley

Top: Peckett-built 0-6-0ST No 618 of 1895 spent its entire career as No 3 at this pit, which was owned before nationalisation by William Harrison Ltd., and connected to the LNWR Norton branch. *19th October 1957*

Brereton Colliery

Centre left: 0-4-2ST *Foggo* was constructed at the Chase Terrace workshops of the Cannock Chase Colliery Co Ltd., from parts supplied in 1946 by Beyer, Peacock & Co of Manchester, to a design which had originated 90 years earlier. By 1954 it was working at the former Brereton Collieries Ltd colliery at Brereton, which was connected to the LNWR at Rugeley Town Station by a 1½ mile branch line. The pit closed in July 1960 and the colliery line to Brereton Sidings (Rugeley Town) followed in 1961. *19th October 1957*

All Stretton Halt

Above: Spotless ex-GWR 'Castle' class 4-6-0 No 5073 *Blenheim* was built at Swindon works in July 1938 as *Cranbrook Castle,* and was one of a dozen examples of this class renamed after RAF aircraft, in 1941. The name *Cranbrook Castle* was later bestowed on No 7030. The locomotive is hauling the 09.10 Liverpool Lime Street and Manchester London Road to Plymouth and Kingswear express. Next to the locomotive, which carries a Shrewsbury (84G) shed plate below the reporting number on its smokebox door, is a 12-wheeled LMS restaurant car. *27th December 1957*

Left: R A Riddles-designed Ministry of Supply 2-8-0 No 90701, allocated to Shrewsbury MPD, works over the joint LNW and GW line with an up freight. Built in January 1945 by the Vulcan Foundry as WD No 79261 and shipped to Europe, it returned from Belgium via Dover in April 1946, and was stored at Richborough in Kent before transfer on loan to the GWR in November of that year. As BR No 90701 the locomotive was withdrawn in November 1962. *27th December 1957*

Colwich Station

Top: A view of the station buildings on the down side, taken from the station approach which led from the A51 road. The entrance for passengers heading north was located under the canopy beside the car. The station, jointly constructed by the LNWR and North Staffordshire Railway, opened in December 1847; the NSR line from Stone was ready by June 1849. Access to the up trains was via a footbridge to the island platform. The former station master's house, to the left of the picture, is still in existence, though the station closed in February 1958 and the buildings and platforms were removed between April and June 1960, prior to remodelling of the layout in preparation for the electrification of the line. *11th January 1958*

Selly Oak Signal Boxes

Right: Standing in the up side coal yard siding is 3F class 0-6-0 No 43435, built at Derby Works in the early 1890's, coupled to what appears to be a 4F's tender. On the 19th January 1958 a new BR Western Region signal box superseded the adjacent Midland Railway one. The commissioning of Saltley Power Signal Box in September 1969 reduced the BR (WR) box to a shunt frame for a short time until it was demolished. At nationalisation in January 1948, control of this former Midland line from Bristol as far as Church Road Junction (45 miles 6 chains), between Five Ways and Selly Oak stations, passed to the Western Region. The regional boundaries were changed in 1958 to a point between Barnt Green and Blackwell (52 miles 40 chains). *13th January 1958*

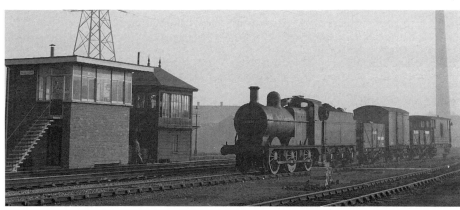

Onibury Station

Opposite page bottom: Viewed looking north. The station buildings, level crossing gates and signal box have all since been demolished. A new signal box, located on the up side, adjacent to the crossing, was built to control traffic over the busy A49 road. Most intermediate stations between Shrewsbury and Hereford on the LNW & GW Joint line were closed on 9th June 1958. *27th December 1957*

Rubery Station

Above left: A joint Great Western & Midland Railways cast iron trespass notice exhibited on the Halesowen Junction to Old Hill line, which opened in March 1878 and lost its regular passenger service in December 1927, although workmen's services continued until 29th August 1958 from Longbridge to Old Hill. Rubery Station was only open from September 1883 to April 1919. *13th January 1958*

Rubery (Frogmill Crossing)

Above right: An unusual Midland Railway signal post carrying two working distant signals. The top arm was worked from Frogmill Crossing frame by the keeper, as an advanced warning to drivers with regard to the position of the gates. The bottom arm was the normal approach distant worked from Rubery Signal Box. The Halesowen to Rubery line closed in January 1964. *13th January 1958*

Halesowen Junction

Left: LMS 'Jubilee' class 4-6-0 No 45654 *Hood*, built at Crewe Works in February 1935 and withdrawn in June 1966, storms westwards on a beautiful frosty morning with the 10.23 (Class B) Birmingham New Street to Gloucester Eastgate service. The line eastwards to Church Road Junction was included in the Western Region until 1958 – *see under 'Selly Oak Signal Boxes' on the previous page.* This explains why Western Region tubular gantries appeared with lower quadrant arms in place of MR/LMS signals. This is the site where Longbridge station was opened on 8th May 1978. *30th January 1958*

Lichfield City

Below: Stanier-designed class 5MT 4-6-0 No 45253, built under contract by Armstrong Whitworth at Newcastle in 1936, slows over the permanent speed restriction through the up platform line before continuing via the South Staffs line to Walsall, and then via the Grand Junction line to Perry Barr North Junction for Smethwick Rolfe Street, with a football excursion from Nottingham Midland for the West Bromwich Albion football ground. The reporting number M956, on the front of the locomotive, indicates to signalmen that this special originated on the Midland Division of the LMR. Full details about the train would be contained in the weekly traffic notice. *8th February 1958*

Minworth (Water Orton)

Right: The Birmingham Tame & Rea Drainage Board operated an extensive 2ft gauge network amongst the sewerage filter beds at this location. Two W G Bagnall-built 0-4-0STs were to be found here, one of which was this machine, No 2088 of 1918. By this time the steam locomotives were not normally in service, the work being done by 4-wheel diesel or petrol driven machines. This locomotive was acquired for the Old-berrow Light Railway at Henley-in-Arden in 1961, but has since moved to the Bredgar & Wormshill Light Railway, near Sittingbourne. *2nd February 1958*

Anglesea Sidings

Centre right: The 12.45 local passenger from Derby Midland to Walsall travels up the South Staffordshire Line headed by a Stanier-designed 2-6-4T No 42488, built at Derby Works in 1937. Passenger services ceased in January 1965, but a single track section from Lichfield City remains in situ to serve the Charrington Oil Terminal at Brown-hills. Hammerwich village church is visible in the background between the signal gantry and the locomotive. *12th February 1958*

Acocks Green and South Yardley

Below: The 10.00 Birmingham Snow Hill to London Paddington approaches the station on the up main on this sunny St Valentine's morning, behind a nicely cleaned ex-GWR 'King' class 4-6-0 No 6001 *King Edward VII*, allocated to Wolverhampton (84A) Stafford Road Depot. *14th February 1958*

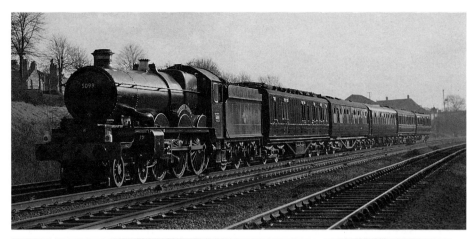

Acocks Green and South Yardley

Left: Approaching on the down main from Olton is 'Castle' class No 5099 *Compton Castle*, hauling part of the Royal train, to Tyseley. It had been used to convey H.R.H. Prince Phillip from Paddington to Solihull to visit the Rover car factory. The two tracks in the foreground, the down and up relief lines, laid in the early 1930s, were taken out of use on 30th June 1968 and removed in the 1970s. No 5099 was built at Swindon Works in May 1946 and withdrawn in February 1963, going to Kings of Norwich for scrapping. *14th February 1958*

Oakengates

Centre left: Ex-Taff Vale Railway 0-6-2T No 190, built at Cardiff West Yard in 1895, became GWR No 581 at the grouping. Upon withdrawal it was sold to the Lilleshall Company in 1932. As access to the works was through Hollinswood Yard sidings, the locomotive was registered by the Railway Executive in 1953 and carried a plate to indicate that it could travel on BR metals. It was scrapped in 1958. *15th February 1958*

Nuneaton Abbey Street

Bottom: LMS-built 3-cylinder Compound No 40933, built in June 1927 and withdrawn the month after this photograph was taken, approaches the station with the 13.45 Birmingham New Street to Yarmouth and Lowestoft, via the Midland & Great Northern Joint line. Services were re-routed via Peterborough following closure of the M&GN in 1959. *11th March 1958*

Burton-on-Trent

Above: Worthington's Brewery employed four steam and six 4-wheeled diesel locomotives at this period although stock was pooled with Bass, Ratcliffe and Gretton from 1960. No 6, a Hudswell Clarke 0-4-0ST (works number 1417 of 1920), is seen here working the internal system. The Brewery Museum at Burton-on-Trent contains No 9, an 0-4-0ST built in 1901 by Neilson & Company at Glasgow (works no 5907). *8th March 1958*

Southam and Long Itchington

Right: The Rugby Portland Cement works operated a 1ft 11½in gauge system utilising four Peckett-built 0-6-0STs. Illustrated here is *Mesozoic,* works no 1327, built in 1913. The other three were *Jurassic, Triassic* and *Liassic. Mesozoic* is now preserved on the Bromyard & Linton Light Railway; *Jurassic* on the Lincolnshire Coast Light Railway at Burgh-le-Marsh and *Triassic* at the Bala Lake Light Railway at Llanuwchllyn. *Liassic* was shipped to Canada in 1959. *9th March 1958*

Nuneaton Abbey Junction

Above: My second request for 'smoke' – the result of my first such request can be seen on page 43 – came after a rather bumpy footplate ride from Birmingham New Street on the 09.35 to Leicester London Road, behind No 40935, an ex-LMS 3-cylinder Compound, built at Derby in 1932 and withdrawn from service in March 1958, and allocated to Bournville (21B) MPD. Before Abbey Street Station closed, all passenger trains took the route over the skew bridge (crossing the WCML) direct to Midland Junction. Abbey Street Station closed on 4th March 1968. *11th March 1958*

Nechells Power Station

Centre left: The Central Electricity Generating Board kept four locomotives at this Birmingham power station, including No 3, an 0-6-0T built by Robert Stephenson & Hawthorn, (works no 7537 of 1949). Now named *Richard III,* it can be seen operating on 'The Battlefield Line' at Shackerstone, Leicestershire, along with sister locomotive works no 7684 of 1951. *11th March 1958*

Longbridge

Left: Abernant, an 0-6-0ST built by Manning Wardle (works number 2015 of 1921), came to the Austin Motor Company from Cardiff Corporation, who had used it on the construction of the Llwynon Reservoir, near Merthy Tydfil. When withdrawn it went on static display in a children's play area at Duddeston, opposite the Carriage & Wagon workshops. Removal to the Birmingham Railway Museum took place in 1989. *16th April 1958*

Longbridge

Right: BMC's former Austin Motor Company works connected with BR metals between Halesowen Junction and Longbridge West. No 5 *Austin*, an 0-6-0T built by Davenport, (works no 2505), for the US Transportation Corps in, 1943, was one of two such locomotives acquired in 1949. It was scrapped in September 1958. *16th April 1958*

Whitmore Station

Centre right: A Manchester London Road and Liverpool Lime Street service to Birmingham New Street – the two portions having combined at Crewe – has come off the troughs and is moving through the closed station on the up fast, having topped the 11 mile climb with gradients between 1 in 177 and 1 in 348. The locomotive is class 5MT 4-6-0 No 44761, built at Crewe in 1947. Whitmore was termed a 'first class' station when the Grand Junction Railway opened in July 1837. Multiple aspect signalling was introduced in July 1961 and overhead line equipment was energised in November 1962. The box closed in October 1961; the station closed for passengers on 4th February 1952 and for goods on 8th June 1965. *19th April 1958*

Madeley Station

Below: Driver H Hobbs of Camden, works the 10.50 London Euston to Blackpool Central and Llandudno along the down fast with rebuilt 'Patriot' class 4-6-0 No 45514 *Holyhead.* Although MAS was introduced in October 1961 Madeley box was retained to control the chord line for merry-go-round coal trains to and from Silverdale Colliery. The station closed to passengers on 4th February 1952 and to goods traffic on 19th August 1963. *19th April 1958*

Victoria Colliery, North Staffordshire

Left: One of the fleet of locomotives formerly owned by the Norton & Biddulph Collieries Ltd was No 11, an 0-6-0ST built by Black, Hawthorn & Company of Gateshead in 1888 (works number 949). A spark arrester has been fitted to the chimney. The last rail traffic out of this colliery was in December 1975. *19th April 1958*

Florence Colliery, North Staffordshire

Centre left: This 0-6-0ST, named *Florence No 2*, was built by W G Bagnall of Stafford in 1953 (works no 3059) for the Coal Board for use at this former Florence Coal & Iron Company pit at Longton. It is hauling an 8-plank internal user wagon: the large white diagonal cross indicating that it was not permitted to run on BR tracks. This locomotive is now on 'The Battlefield Line' at Shackerstone, near Market Bosworth in Leicestershire. *19th April 1958*

Worcester Shrub Hill Station

Below: A short express arrives from Hereford behind ex-GWR 4-cylinder 'Castle' class 4-6-0 No 5012 *Berry Pomeroy Castle*. The addition of a restaurant car and perhaps as many as five coaches would take place here before the train worked forward to Oxford, Reading and London Paddington. No 5012 was built at Swindon Works in July 1927 and withdrawn in April 1962. Disposal for scrap was to J Cashmore's yard at Newport. *26th April 1958*

Corby

Right: Andrew Barclay 0-6-0ST No 5 *Ironworks No 1*, built at Kilmarnock in 1911 (works number 1241), is seen in the Stewart & Lloyds steel works complex. Behind the locomotive is a barrier wagon to distance the crew from the intense heat of the molten metal in the cauldron wagons, being shunted in this view. *17th May 1958*

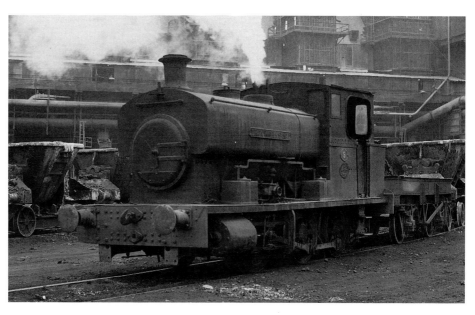

Ketton Cement Company sidings

Centre right: No 4, a smart 0-4-0ST built by Hawthorn Leslie in 1920 (works no 3479), shunts internal user wagons at this location between Manton Junction and Stamford on the Leicester to Peterborough line . This site still generates railborne traffic today. *17th May 1958*

Coventry Station

Below: The old station had only two platforms with two through middle roads. Here Stanier 2P 0-4-4T No 41902, one of a class of 10 machines built at Derby, originally numbered 6400 to 6409, and introduced in 1932, is working a Nuneaton Trent Valley to Leamington Avenue service. No 41902 was allocated to Warwick (2C) MPD at this time. The greater part of the old station at Coventry was demolished between January and March 1960. *20th May 1958*

Wigginton Troughs

Above: A fully-fitted freight from Leeds to Westerleigh Sidings travels over the down-line trough towards Tamworth High Level, headed by BR Standard class 9F 2-10-0 No 92165, allocated to Saltley (21A) MPD. Built at Crewe Works in April 1958 and fitted with an American-designed Berkeley mechanical stoker, one of only three BR locomotives to be so equipped, it was withdrawn in March 1968 and sold for scrap to Cashmores at Newport. *22nd June 1958*

Fairford Station

Below: The 18.10 to Oxford awaits departure time behind ex-GWR 0-6-0PT No 7412. In order to return chimney first the locomotive has used the turntable here. The small shed was still in use. This line, which left the main line at Witney Junction (Yarnton), closed to passengers in June 1962 and to freight in 1965. The branch ran across the runway at RAF Fairford, an airfield occupied at the time by units of the United States Air Force. *5th July 1958*

Wolverton – 52½mp WCML

Above left: CD7, one of the former LNWR Ramsbottom/Webb 0-6-0STs employed as a Carriage Department shunter, takes a LCGB special from Wolverton to Newport Pagnell along the WCML's up slow. *Above right:* Two other survivors of the class, CD8 and CD3, at Wolverton Station on the same day. *28th June 1958*

Birmingham Snow Hill Station

Below: During the West Midlands' industrial fortnight, (the last week of July and the first week of August), daily excursions were run to different destinations to cater for those families not holidaying away from home. Featured here awaiting departure from Platform 2, with a trip to Rhyl is former GWR 4-6-0 No 7821 *Ditcheat Manor*. This working necessitated a reversal and change of engine at Chester. The locomotive is now in preservation. *29th July 1958*

Radstock North

Above: A special relief train, reporting number W734, running from Coventry to Bournemouth West, heads south behind 4-4-0 40700, piloting BR Standard 4-6-0 No 73051. *26th July 1958*

Below: This picture now strikes me as a wonderful evocation of the late 1950s. Motorists sit at the first of Radstock's two level crossings on the A367 while the first down stopping train of the day, from Bath Green Park to Templecombe, departs at 07.25 behind BR

Standard class 4MT 2-6-0 No 76017, built at Horwich in June 1953 and now preserved on the Mid-Hants Railway. *26th July 1958*

Midsomer Norton

Above: The 08.00 Bristol Temple Meads to Bournemouth West passes over the A362 road on a mile-long climb at 1 in 50, headed by ex-LMS 4-4-0 No 40698. The train engine is BR Standard class 5MT 4-6-0 No 73047. *26th July 1958*

Midsomer Norton South Station

Above: The 12.20 relief from Bournemouth West to Derby Midland is hauled by 7F 2-8-0 No 53810, one of eleven built, the first six at Derby in 1914, the remainder by Robert Stephenson & Co in 1925. Due to heavy Saturday traffic, these goods engines were often pressed into passenger service. *26th July 1958*

Radstock

Below: BR Standard class 5MT No 73071, hauls a rake of Southern Region stock which forms the 09.55 Bath Green Park to Bournemouth West stopping service. Note that the locomotive is attached to a flush sided BR1C tender, the maximum capacity of which was 9 tons of coal and 4725 gallons of water. *26th July 1958*

Midsomer Norton South Station

Above: A Cleethorpes to Bournemouth West train breasts the 1 in 50 climb with '2P' 4-4-0 No 40696 piloting Southern Railway 'West Country' 4-6-2 No 34099 *Lynmouth,* built at Eastleigh in 1949. The S&D Joint line had its own distinctive lamp codes. That for passenger trains, as shown here, was one lamp under the chimney and one over the right buffer. *26th July 1958*

Radstock West

Below left: Former GWR 5700 class 0-6-0PT No 4636 heads a morning Frome to Bristol Temple Meads local passenger service. The S&D Joint line, under which the train will soon pass, can be seen behind the locomotive. Passenger services ceased in November 1959 and freight services lasted until November 1963. *26th July 1958*

Radstock shed

Above: This was home to two 4-wheeled Sentinel locomotives used to shunt the Radstock Colliery branches. Here, No 47191, built in 1929, rests between duties. *26th July 1958*

Birmingham Snow Hill North

Above: GWR Railcar No 13, built in 1936 by the Gloucester Carriage and Wagon Company, runs into No 4 bay platform to form the 09.55 departure for all stations to Dudley. Snow Hill North Signal Box, visible behind the railcar, was opened in 1910 with 224 levers, described as electric power signalling by makers Siemens. *29th July 1958*

Swadlincote Station

Below: The 10.25 (SO) Blackpool North to Leicester London Road, is headed by former LMS 0-6-0 No 44148, allocated to Coalville (15D) Motive Power Depot. It pilots Stanier class 5 4-6-0 No 45101, built by Vulcan Foundry in 1935. This branch, off the Leicester to Burton line, opened to Swadlincote in 1864 and was extended to Woodville in 1883, from where it was continued back to the main line in 1884 to form a loop. Regular service over the loop was withdrawn on 6th October 1947, though Saturday trains ran until 8th September 1962. Complete closure came in March 1964, although it was used for wagon storage until August 1968. *2nd August 1958*

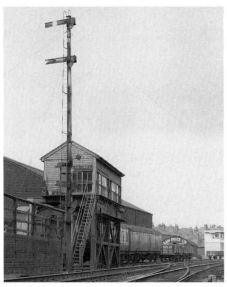

Smethwick Rolfe Street Signal Box

Left: This LNWR signal box, an 'F'-size cabin with 36 levers, built in 1889 for £906, was elevated over the horse dock to the north of Rolfe Street bridge, on the down side. The LNWR co-acting lower quadrant arms (the distants were controlled from Galton Junc), were retained until the new LM Region box, 150 yards north, was opened in April 1960, at which time they were replaced by colour lights. Due to the severe curve approaching the station, early sighting was given to drivers by the upper arms, elevated high above the bridge and buildings. For drivers held at the platform the lower arms were in view. These have been cut back to clear the post and rail fence, when lowered. Multiple aspect signalling, controlled from the New Street Power Signal Box, was introduced in January 1966. *29th July 1958*

Murrow West Crossing

Centre left: The M&GN Joint single line which closed on 28th February 1959, crossed the GN&GE Joint double tracked line from Spalding to March on the level at Murrow West Crossing. A local passenger train bound for Peterborough headed by No 43108, a class 4MT 2-6-0 built at Doncaster Works in May 1951 and withdrawn in November 1965, runs over the crossing, which was itself removed in October 1965. *5th August 1958*

Pleck Station

Below: A view of the distinctive station building on the Wednesbury road, which was demolished in September 1972. The station opened in October 1881 and closed in November 1958. *13th August 1958*

Bourne Station and MPD

Bottom left: Ex-LMS 2-6-0 No 43066 calls with the 09.55 Saxby to Kings Lynn. In the background, Bourne West Signal Box can be seen to the left, whilst the disused former Great Northern Railway motive power depot is visible on the right. This building, seen from another angle *(bottom right)* had lain empty for several years before finally being demolished in the 1960s. Its 60ft turntable was moved initially to Peterborough but was bought by the Nene Valley Railway in 1977 and lengthened to 70ft. *Both photographs 5th August 1958*

Twenty Station

Right: A view of this Midland & Great Northern station and signal box, looking west. The M&GN system consisted of 125 route miles of which 80 were single track. Situated between Bourne and Spalding, this was one of the many isolated country stations to close with the system on 28th February 1959. *5th August 1958*

Pleck Station

Below: This was situated on the connecting line between Pleck Junction and Darlaston Junction, which opened in November 1881 and closed in November 1958. Here the 10.50 Wolverhampton High Level to Walsall push-pull service worked by ex-LMS 2-6-2T No 41225, built at Crewe in 1948, prepares to depart. *13th August 1958*

Fleet Station, M&GNR

Above: GNR Class J6 0-6-0 No 64191 calls with a local from Kings Lynn to Spalding Town. Only one platform was built as the line was single, the level crossing (off picture, left) was controlled by a signal box until November 1957, when it was replaced by a ground frame. *5th August 1958*

Spalding Town Station

Above: A general view of the station from the main road footbridge. Ex-GNR J class 0-6-0 No 64191 stands in the bay with the 12.20 to Kings Lynn, while an ex-LMS 0-6-0 can be seen in the centre platform. Remodelling of the layout and elimination of semaphore signalling took place in 1984. *5th August 1958*

Gedney Station

Top left: A view towards Spalding. The line was originally single, but a passing loop was installed in May 1897 which required the re-siting of the signal box and construction of an additional platform. *5th August 1958*

Spalding Town Station

Above: The first railway into Spalding was the Great Northern Peterborough to Lincoln line in 1847. This was followed by the Bourne to Sutton Bridge route and the GN/GE Joint line to March, in 1867. In its heyday a very busy exchange station with seven platforms, and an engine shed which closed in March 1960. Today, only the Sleaford to Peterborough line retains a passenger service. *5th August 1958*

Weston Station

Top right: A fairly typical M&GN station – with an impressive building on the platform, no siding accommodation or visible habitation in sight – and a road crossing to the village over a mile away! This view looks towards Spalding. *5th August 1958*

Holbeach Station

Left: Reached by the Norwich & Spalding Railway in 1858 and approached from both sides by a single line, a passing loop was provided in 1890. The East Signal Box, illustrated here, controlled the level crossing at the South Lynn end and was not demolished until April 1966. The West Signal Box at the Spalding end controlled access to the goods yard. The loop was closed in February 1964. *5th August 1958*

Shrewsbury Station

Above: Former GWR No 5927 *Guild Hall*, bearing a Tyseley (84E) shed plate, arrives with a Birkenhead Woodside to London Paddington express. *17th August 1958*

Left: Afternoon arrivals include a service from the West Country to Manchester in Platform 4, behind ex-GWR 'Hall' No 6956 *Mottram Hall*, built at Swindon in March 1943, and allocated at this time to Wolverhampton Stafford Road (84A) motive power depot. Ex-LMS 'Jubilee' No 45578 *United Provinces*, taking water in the middle road, will take the train on to Manchester. In Platform 3 stands a train which has arrived from Swansea over the Central Wales line, worked in by Stanier class 8F 2-8-0 No 48730, allocated to Swansea Victoria (87K) MPD. The Central Wales line was one of the few places where these former LMR freight workhorses could regularly be seen on passenger duties. *17th August 1958*

Birmingham Snow Hill, South Signal Box

Right: A track-side view of 'The Cornishman' standing in Platform No 7 and a 0-6-0PT on the up through. Opened in 1910, Snow Hill South Box had a 96-lever miniature frame supplied by Siemens. Snow Hill power signal box replaced both the north and south boxes in September 1960. *15th August 1958*

Longbridge Station (No 3 platform)

Centre left: The GWR line between Old Hill and Halesowen lost its regular passenger service in December 1927. The Halesowen to Northfield southern extension of this line, owned jointly by the Midland and the Great Western, lost its passenger service as early as 1919. However, a non-timetabled workmen's train survived for another 30 years, to serve the car factory at Longbridge. Here, the very last 17.40 for Hunnington, Halesowen and Old Hill, prepares to leave Longbridge behind Stourbridge (84F) allocated 0-6-0PT No 7430. Line closure north of Longbridge West came in 1964. *29th August 1958*

Handsworth Wood

Centre right: Rebuilt 4-6-0 'Royal Scot' class No 46118 *Royal Welsh Fusilier* between Soho East Junction and Perry Barr West Junction with empty stock that will form the 11.25 Birmingham New Street to Glasgow Central. *29th August 1958*

Birmingham Snow Hill Station

Bottom: On the down through (north end) prior to working a SLS special to Swindon Works is prototype 'Hall' No 4900 *Saint Martin*, a 1924 Collett rebuild of 'Saint' No 2925, with side window cab, 6ft driving wheels and outside steam pipes. *7th September 1958*

Swindon Works

Top, left: No 18000, Britain's first main line gas-turbine locomotive, was ordered by the GWR from Brown Boveri, a Swiss company, in 1940, eight years prior to nationalisation. It was constructed to an established Swiss design at Winterthur (works no 3977) and delivered in 1949, painted in the main line black and silver livery of that era. It underwent extensive testing on the Paddington to Bristol and West of England routes until withdrawal in 1960. It was sold back to its makers in 1963 and shipped to Switzerland the following year. It was later used as a Union International de Chemin de Fers (UIC) test vehicle but was returned from Vienna for preservation at the Railway Age site at Crewe in 1994. *13th September 1958*

Daventry Station

Centre: Ivatt 2-6-2T 41228, which was built at Crewe Works in October 1948 and withdrawn in June 1964, calls with the 14.58 (SO) from Leamington Spa Avenue to Northampton Castle on the last day of passenger services between Marton Junction and Weedon. *13th September 1958*

Weedon Station – 69½ mp WCML

Left: The 15.45 London Euston to Manchester London Road passes through this WCML station, headed by former LMS 'Royal Scot' class 4-6-0 No 46157 *The Royal Artilleryman*, on the last day that Weedon Station was open. The bay behind the platform buildings was used by the Leamington Spa Avenue services which terminated here. *13th September 1958*

Shrewsbury Abbey Station

Right: The Shropshire & Montgomeryshire Light Railway ran from Shrewsbury via Kinnerley Junction to Llanymynech and Criggion. The Army utilised the system for many years using Dean 0-6-0s and later, Ministry of Supply 0-6-0STs. Here, the Stephenson Locomotive Society have organised a special headed by WD (War Department) 0-6-0ST No 188, (Vulcan Foundry works No 5284 of 1945). The line closed in 1960, except for a short section servicing an oil terminal at Abbey Foregate, which survived until 1990. Shrewsbury Abbey, the medieval home of the fictitious detective Brother Cadfael, is across the road, beyond its eponymous station. *14th September 1958*

Kinnerley MOD Railway Shed

Above: Situated on the former Shropshire & Montgomeryshire Light Railway which ran from Shrewbury Abbey Street Station, Ministry of Supply locomotives in view are: No 125 built in 1943 by Robert Stephenson & Hawthorn (works No 7099), in the shed; No 141 built by Hunslet (works No 3195) of 1944, in the centre; and on the right No 143 built by W G Bagnall (works No 2740). *14th September 1958*

Birmingham Snow Hill Station

Right: The Talyllyn Railway Society annual special was worked between London Paddington and Shrewsbury, on this occasion by former LMS 3-cylinder Compound 4-4-0 No 41123, sporting a Gloucester Barnwood (85E) shed plate. *27th September 1958*

Bristol Temple Meads Station

Above: GWR Hawksworth designed 'County' class 4-6-0 No 1000 *County of Middlesex* heads a local passenger service to Weston-Super-Mare. The class consisted of 30 locomotives, all built prior to Nationalisation. No 1000 was built in August 1945, withdrawn in July 1964 and scrapped at Cashmores, Newport. This was the only locomotive of the class to be fitted with a double chimney from the outset. *1st October 1958*

Bristol Bath Road MPD

Below: GWR 'King' class locomotive No 6003 *King George IV* moves around the shed yard before being coaled up prior to working an afternoon express to London Paddington. It will be noticed that a chalked reporting number 018 has been drawn on the smoke box door in lieu of the usual Western practice of metal numbers slotted into a frame. This reporting number was its previous working, the 12.30am newspaper train from Paddington. *1st October 1958*

Bloxwich signal boxes

Above left: The LNWR signal box was replaced by one of BR design in March 1959. The level crossing gates have since been replaced by lifting barriers, operated from the signal box. The line opened in February 1858 between Ryecroft Junction and Cannock and although passenger services ceased in January 1965, a revived service between Walsall and Hednesford was reinstated in April 1989. When engineering works block the Grand Junction route between Bushbury Junction at Wolverhampton, and Stafford, this line is used as a diversion. It also carries coal traffic from collieries in the East Midlands to the Rugeley Power Station. *21st January 1959*

Spalding Motive Power Depot

Top right: This small M&GN Joint two road shed, a sub-shed of New England (35A) MPD at Peterborough, was used until March 1960. It was demolished and the site cleared in 1965. *21st February 1959*

Spalding Town Station

Centre right: LNER K3 class 2-6-0 No 61850 in ex-works condition, allocated to Sheffield Darnall (41A), passes through with a partially fitted freight. Track rationalisation and resignalling in 1984 resulted in the elimination of the semaphore signals seen in the picture. *21st February 1959*

Windsor Street (Birmingham) Gas Works

Bottom right: Built in 1930 by Peckett, works number 1812, this 0-4-0ST No 4 *Windsor* was one of this maker's W6 Special class, with cut-down cab and boiler mountings, for working where clearances were limited. Registered with the Railway Executive in 1952 to enable it to work over BR tracks in the vicinity of the works, it was scrapped in 1969. The Gas Works closed in 1974. *28th February 1959*

Nechells Gas Works Birmingham

Left: In the late 1950s, as many as seven locomotives were employed at this works, which had been owned by the City of Birmingham Corporation Gas Department until May 1949. Pictured here is No 8, an 0-4-0ST built by Andrew Barclay (works No 1992 of 1932) and scrapped in January 1964. Interestingly, this is a rebuilt locomotive using the frames from the old No.7 (Andrew Barclay No 1797 of 1924). The connection to the works, which closed in 1969, was off the Midland line at Washwood Heath.
28th February 1959

Aston Station

Below: Former LMS class 5MT No 45318, built by Armstrong Whitworth in 1937, works the empty stock of a football special from Skipton to Witton (the station for Aston Villa's ground), to Vauxhall carriage sidings – note the Central Division special reporting number, C740. Aston No 2 Signal Box was abolished on the 4th July 1966 with the introduction of multipal aspect signalling, controlled from Birmingham New Street Signal Box. Energisation of overhead line equipment took place in August 1966. The wooden platforms were replaced with standard units; the down side in October 1990 and the up side in August 1992.
28th February 1959

Nechells Gas Works, Birmingham

Above: Nechells Gas Works No 10 was a 200hp vertical-boilered locomotive supplied new in 1956 by Sentinel of Shrewsbury (works No 9617). It was scrapped in March 1968. *28th February 1959*

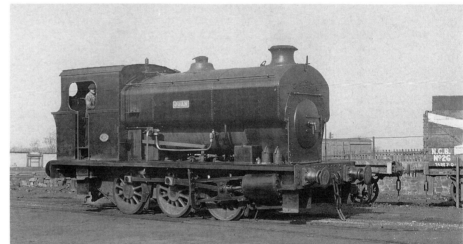

Arley Colliery

Centre right: Joan, an 0-6-0ST built by Avonside Engineering Company of Bristol (works No 2048 of 1932) was delivered new to the Arley Colliery Co Ltd and remained at the pit, which was alongside the LNWR Birmingham-Nuneaton line, until 1968. *1st March 1959*

Coventry Colliery

Right: Posing in front of the colliery's winding gear is 0-6-0ST *Coventry No 4,* built by Peckett of Bristol in 1927 (works No 1748). Supplied new to the colliery, it was scrapped on site, in November 1969. The colliery at Keresley, to the north of the city, was reached by a 2 mile branch from the LNWR Coventry-Nuneaton line. *1st March 1959*

Ansley Hall Colliery

Left: 0-4-0ST *Ansley Hall* built by Peckett in 1905, (works No 991), and rebuilt in 1939, was scrapped at Binley Colliery in August 1963. Binley Colliery was on the eastern outskirts of Coventry, but Ansley Hall (formerly owned by Ansley Hall Coal & Iron Co Ltd) was reached via a branch from Stockingford, on the Birmingham to Nuneaton line. *1st March 1959*

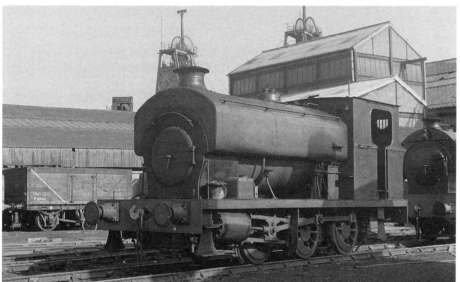

Haunchwood Colliery

Centre left: This North Warwickshire pit was also situated alongside the Birmingham to Nuneaton line, but just to the west of Stockingford. Delivered new here by Avonside Engine Co of Bristol in 1922 (works No 1883) was this 0-6-0ST. The colliery closed in March 1967 and the locomotive was transferred to Arley Colliery. *1st March 1959*

North Warwickshire Colliery

Below: Named Pooley Hall until 1951, this colliery closed in April 1965. The full locomotive fleet is lined up outside the shed for a Sunday visit by members of the Birmingham Locomotive Club. All are 0-4-0STs: *Kia Ora*, Peckett No 1173 of 1912; *Kapai*, also a Peckett, works No 1532 of 1920; and *Cowburn*, a Hunslet, works No 544 of 1891. They were scrapped in 1966. The outlet for rail traffic was onto the West Coast main line between Polesworth and Marshall's Sidings. *1st March 1959*

Baddesley Colliery

Above: One of only four Garratts supplied to industrial concerns in Britain, this Beyer Peacock 0-4-4-0, No 6841, built in 1937 and named *William Francis,* is now preserved. Following withdrawal in 1965, it went to the Bressingham Steam Museum in Norfolk. Until 1972 the colliery was reached via a steeply graded 1½ mile line from sidings on the WCML, north of Atherstone, over an ungated crossing on the A5. *1st March 1959*

Newdigate Colliery

Centre right: A branch led from the Coventry to Nuneaton line, south of Bedworth, to this colliery. 0-6-0ST No 3, built in 1922 by Peckett of Bristol (works No 1586) came here new and was scrapped here in June 1968. *1st March 1959*

Coventry Colliery

Bottom right: 0-6-0T *Coventry No 5,* built by Sharp Stewart in 1888 (works No 3449), was originally Barry Railway No 1 of Class A, becoming GWR No 699. It was sold to Warwickshire Coal Co Ltd in 1933 for use at the colliery and was scrapped on site in March 1962. *1st March 1959*

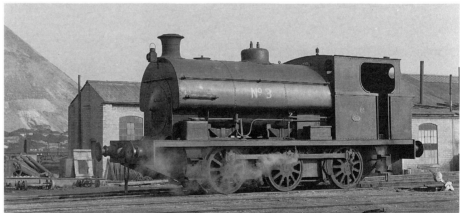

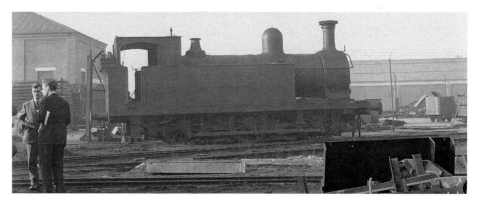

Haunchwood Colliery

Left: The National Coal Board acquired a number of the Austerity 0-6-0ST locos built for the Ministry of Supply and in the post-war period more were supplied new. No 1 at Haunchwood was built by the Hunslet Engine Company of Leeds (works No 3828) in 1955. It was sold for scrap in October 1967. The colliery was served by a connection off the Midland line between Arley Tunnel and Stockingford. *1st March 1959*

Tamworth Low Level Station

Below: Former LMS rebuilt 'Royal Scot' class 4-6-0 No 46101 *Royal Scots Grey* passes on the up fast through the original station, opened in 1847. Rebuilding of the station commenced in 1960 and was completed two years later. The locomotive was rebuilt in November 1945 and withdrawn from service in September 1963. The train is 'The Emerald Isle', the 07.30 Holyhead to London Euston. The signal box to the left of the picture, originally No 2, is still in use today. *5th March 1959*

Olton Station

Top left: GWR 'Castle' class No 5061 *Earl of Birkenhead*, built at Swindon in June 1937 and withdrawn in September 1962 is seen here working a Paddington to Birkenhead express near Olton on the outskirts of Birmingham between Tyseley and Solihull. The up and down relief lines between Small Heath South and Solihull were taken out of service in June 1968. The GWR used the term relief lines for the extra tracks which would have been referred to as the slow or goods lines on the London Midland Region. *5th March 1959*

Top right: Former GWR 'Castle' class 4-6-0 No 5046 *Earl Cawdor*, is here working the up 15.00 Birmingham Snow Hill to London Paddington express. *5th March 1959*

Brindley Heath Station

Below: A view looking towards Rugeley with Moors Gorse level crossing in the distance. The station was opened in August 1939 to serve the vast Royal Air Force training camp on Cannock Chase. Closure of the station came in April 1959. The crossing cottage remains but the protecting signals have been removed. *15th March 1959*

Birmingham Snow Hill

Bottom The stock of 'The Cornishman', the 09.40 from Snow Hill runs into Platforms 7/8. Behind the locomotive is the North Signal Box. Opened in 1910, this had a 224 lever frame. The Siemens-equipped North and South boxes were replaced by a new power box which is seen under construction in this view. Built at Swindon Works in May 1937 'Castle' class 4-6-0 No 5059 *Earl of St Aldwyn* was withdrawn in June 1962 and cut up at Swindon Works. *16th March 1959*

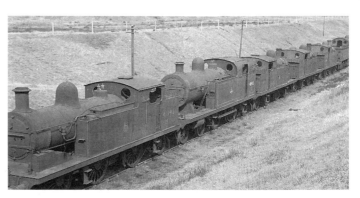

Kibworth North

Top left: The 10.25 Manchester Central to London St. Pancras heads south behind Metropolitan-Vickers 1200 hp Co-Bo's Nos D5700, built in July 1958, and D5710, built in February 1959. Both were withdrawn in September 1967 and scrapped by J. McWilliam at Shettleton in 1968. Note escaping steam from the steam heating boiler on the roof of the second locomotive. One of the class, D5705 is preserved on the Peak Railway. *21st March 1959*

Over Wharton Branch

Top right: Several locations were utilzed to store withdrawn locomotives, including this one in Cheshire, where over 30 await the call to Crewe Works to be cut up. This picture shows London Tilbury & Southend 0-6-2Ts and one 4-4-2T. *30th March 1959*

Norton Bridge Junction Signal box

Above: This box closed in December 1960 and a new BR version opened, 135 yards nearer Stafford on the up side of the tracks – adjacent to the station. Multiple aspect signalling was introduced in July 1961 and this newer signal box remains to control the area. The train engine hauling the express on the down fast is No 46100 *Royal Scot*, which was preserved at Bressingham Gardens, Diss, Norfolk, when it was withdrawn in October 1962. The pilot engine is 'Jubilee' class 4-6-0 No 45722 *Defence,* built in August 1936 and withdrawn in November 1962. *31st March 1959*

Bagnall Wharf – WCML 141½ mp

LMS rebuilt 'Royal Scot' class 4-6-0 No 46128 *The Lovat Scouts* heads an up fast express. The yard to the left contained 20 locomotives awaiting scrapping at Crewe Works. Note the permanent way gang intent on crossing fettling, and trying to manipulate a wheel barrow in the down fast while an express roars by. No look-out man, no HV vests – what a Health and Safety nightmare! *31st March 1959*

Standon Bridge Signal Box

Above: Situated south of the station and between the fast and slow lines, with the introduction of multiple aspect signalling in October 1961 the box was closed and later demolished. Overhead line equipment between Basford Hall and Stafford was energised in November 1961. The station was closed to passengers on 4th February 1952 and to goods traffic on 4th January 1965. Ex-LMS class 5 4-6-0 No 45093, built in April 1935 by the Vulcan Foundry at Newton-le-Willows and withdrawn in November 1965, passes on the up fast with a special express working. *31st March 1959*

Alsop-en-le-Dale Station

Centre right: Two goods trains, both hauled by LNWR G2 0-8-0 locomotives, pass in the station loop on the line between Ashbourne and Buxton. Passenger services began in 1899 and ceased in November 1954; goods services ceased in June 1964. The track bed has since been turned into a cycle trail and the signal box is a warden's post. *4th April 1959*

Mexborough MPD

Right: Great Central Railway J11 class 0-6-0, No 64377, introduced by J G Robinson in 1901, was built by the Vulcan Foundry (works No 1938) in 1904. *12th April 1959*

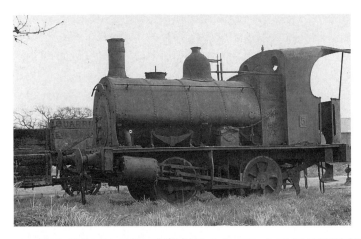

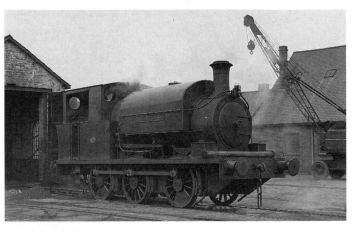

Bardon Hill

Top left: No 5, an 0-4-0ST was built by the Coalbrookdale Company at Ironbridge in 1865. It worked at Coalbrookdale until 1932 until sold to Bardon Hill Quarries where it worked until 1956. The locomotive was subsequently preserved and moved in 1959 to permanent display at the Iron-bridge Gorge Museum, to mark the 250th anniversary of the Coalbrookdale Company. *18th April 1959*

Snibston Colliery, Coalville

Top right: This colliery, to the north-west of the town, and with a connection to the MR Burton to Leicester line, was sunk in 1832 by George and Robert Stephenson. It is now part of the Snibston Discovery Park, a sci-ence and industry museum. NCB East Midlands Area 0-6-0ST *Snibston II*, built by Manning Wardle in 1921 (works No 2007) stands outside the shed, which nowadays houses three of the museum's locomotives. Sadly, No 2007 did not survive to be part of the display here. *16th April 1959*

Burton-on-Trent

Centre left: A rear view of Bass, Ratcliffe and Gretton Breweries' No 3, an 0-4-0ST, built locally by Thornewill & Warham Ltd of New Street Works, Burton-on-Trent (works No 609) – the last of 12 locos supplied by this firm to the Bass Breweries. *16th April 1959*

Whitwick Colliery, Coalville

Left: North-east of Coalville, between the MR Leicester to Swannington line and the LNWR line to Loughborough, was Whitwick Colliery. Over the years there were four Hunslet 0-6-0STs here, the last of which, No 4, (works number 845), built at Leeds in 1902, awaits the scrapping that took place in 1960. *18th April 1959*

Burton-on-Trent

Right: No 11, built by Neilson Reid & Co in 1898, (works number 5568), was one of the 0-4-0STs employed by Bass, Ratcliffe and Gretton Breweries on the miles of internal sidings around the breweries. Note the 4-link coupling, designed to ease coupling and uncoupling on the tight curves. Sister locomotive No 9 (Neilson Reid No 5907 of 1901) is displayed in the Bass Museum. *18th April 1959*

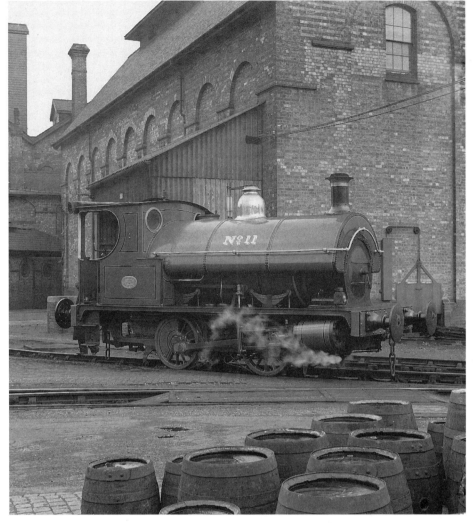

Bordesley Station

Below: Former GWR 2-6-2T No 4126 pilots 0-6-2T No 6667 on the down main with a goods bound for Hockley. At this time, due to bridge renewal work outside Snow Hill tunnel, where the line crossed over the four-track section leading into New Street, a severe temporary speed restriction was imposed. This came on top of the steep gradient through the tunnel and led to all goods and some passenger trains being double-headed while the speed restriction lasted. *25th April 1959*

Selly Oak

Left: BR Standard class 5MT 4-6-0 No 73065 built at Derby Works in October 1954, and withdrawn in July 1967, pilots former LMS 'Jubilee' class 4-6-0 No 45648 *Wemyss*, built at Crewe Works in January 1935 and withdrawn in February 1963, on the 08.15 Newcastle to Cardiff. The Queen Elizabeth hospital is in the background. This section of the line between Birmingham New Street and Kings Norton via Selly Oak opened in April 1876 and is known as the West Surburban Line. *2nd May 1959*

University Station

Above: Former LMS 'Jubilee' class 4-6-0 No 45682 *Trafalgar*, built at Crewe works in January 1936 and withdrawn in June 1964, passes the site where University Station was opened on 8th May 1978, adjacent to the Queen Elizabeth hospital. On the same date two other new stations were opened at Five Ways and Longbridge. The 'Jubilee' is hauling the 10.43 Sheffield Midland to Bristol Temple Meads express. *2nd May 1959*

Birmingham New Street Station

Left: The 11.20 departure for Glasgow and Edinburgh stands at the south end of No 3 platform headed by ex-LMS rebuilt 'Patriot' Class 4-6-0 No 45528, which began life as an LNWR 'Claughton'. The name *R.E.M.E.* (Royal Electrical & Mechanical Engineers) was given to No 45528 late in life, in 1960, just three years before it was withdrawn. The working of this train started as an empty stock movement from Vauxhall Sidings going via Perry Barr and Soho East and South junctions into New Street Station. It followed the Grand Junction line to Wolverhampton High Level. *2nd May 1959*

Stamford Town Station

Right: Passenger trains on the last day of service on the line from Stamford Town to Essendine were entrusted to an ex-Manchester, Sheffield & Lincolnshire Railway 0-6-2T to a design which was introduced in 1891. N5 class No 69292 stands with the 13.08 departure. The branch was opened in 1856. Note the ceremonial wreath around the chimney and chalked inscription above the buffer beam to mark the passing of the branch line.
13th June 1959

Kings Norton Station

Above: Ex-LMS 2-8-0 No 48607, built in September 1943 and withdrawn in August 1965, takes the Camp Hill line through platform 3 with an empty mineral wagon train for Washward Heath up sidings. This line was opened in 1840 by the Birmingham & Gloucester Railway and led to a terminus at Curzon Street in the city. This station was replaced by New Street in 1884. *18th June 1959*

Barnt Green Single Line Junction Signal box

Right: The driver of 4MT 2-6-0 No 43049, built at Horwich Works in November 1949; takes the single line token from the signalman for the 5 miles to Redditch while working tender first, the 12.57 Birmingham New Street to Ashchurch passenger service. The line beyond Redditch was closed completely in July 1964, passenger services having ceased in June 1963. The signal box was abolished with the introduction of stage 3B of the Saltley power signal box multiple aspect signalling scheme. Electrification was completed in June 1992 and full EMU services commenced over the branch in July of the following year. *18th June 1959*

Barnt Green Station

Former Midland Railway 0-6-0 class 4 No 43985, allocated to Saltley (21A) and built in 1921 by Armstrong Whitworth at Newcastle-upon-Tyne. Note the reversing lever above the centre splasher indicating this to be a right hand drive locomotive. The train is proceeding towards the Lickey incline. The first eight vans had been collected from Cadbury's sidings at Bournville. *18th June 1959*

Rowington Troughs – 114¹/₂ mp

Below: BR Standard class 9F 2-10-0 No 92151, built at Crewe Works in November 1957 and withdrawn in April 1967, works a partially fitted up goods from Washwood Heath Sidings. The GWR operated 15 sets of troughs throughout its system; those at Rowington, between Hatton and Lapworth, were 560 yards in length and in operation from October 1899 until April 1967. *20th June 1959*

Penns Station

Right: The Walsall to Birmingham New Street passenger service via the Midland Railway route ceased in January 1965. Here a short engineers train headed by former Midland Railway 0-6-0 No 58124, then allocated to Bushbury (3B) MPD, travels towards Park Lane Junction.
23rd June 1959

Arley and Fillongley Station

Below: Class 4F 0-6-0 No 44332, allocated to Burton (17B) MPD, moves a train of 16-ton mineral wagons from Hams Hall Power Station to Coalville. Arley station opened with the line in November 1864. It closed to passengers on 7th November 1960 and to goods on 4th January 1965. Due to the low height of the platforms, steps were provided to assist passengers on and off trains. A pair of these can be seen to the left of the picture. *24th June 1959*

Birmingham New Street Station

Above: The 07.40 Bristol Temple Meads to Bradford Foster Square stands at No.7 platform headed by BR Standard class 5MT 4-6-0 No 73068, built at Derby Works in October 1954 and withdrawn in December 1965. Traces of its lined green livery can be seen under the grime. The locomotive bears a Yeovil (82E) shed plate. *24th June 1959*

Retford South Junction

Left: Former LNER class A3 4-6-2 No 60049, was built at Doncaster Works in September 1924 as No 2548 *Galtee More*. It is seen arriving at the station with a Newcastle-bound express from Kings Cross and is obviously of great interest to the spotters gathered on No 1 platform. This locomotive was eventually withdrawn in December 1962. *11th July 1959*

Radcliffe-on-Trent

Right: The 09.25 Derby Friargate to Sutton-on-Sea and Mablethorpe travels over what today is a two-track section. The two centre lines have been removed leaving the one on which the train is running and that nearest the camera. The latter has been used by the BR Technical Centre at Derby as a test-bed for different types of track and permanent way components. The ex-LNER locomotive heading the train is a K2 class 2-6-0 No 61752 introduced by H N Gresley in 1914 on the Great Northern Railway.
25th July 1959

Retford South Junction – ECML

Centre right: A two-car Derby-built Diesel Multiple Unit in use on a Newark to Doncaster service, enters the station. The lines from Lincoln and Gainsborough to Worksop and Sheffield cross under the leading vehicle. *11th July 1959*

Colwich – 126½ mp

Below: 'The Red Rose' would not be in the care of this combination had an 8P class locomotive been available at Camden (1B) MPD. Heading along the down fast is former LMS class 5MT No 45256, built by Armstrong Whitworth in 1936, whilst the train engine is rebuilt 'Royal Scot' class No 46123 *Royal Irish Fusilier*. The down fast between Armitage and Colwich Junction became the down slow in December 1961 and vice versa. *4th August 1959*

Great Ponton – 103 mp ECML

Top: A 'class C' express goods heads south up the 1 in 200 gradient towards Stoke Tunnel hauled by BR Standard class 9F 2-10-0 No 92198. This locomotive was built at Swindon Works in October 1958, withdrawn in August 1964 and scrapped by T W Ward at Beighton. *8th August 1959*

Great Ponton

Above: Former LNER 4-6-2 class A4 No 60014 *Silver Link*, the first streamlined A4 built at Doncaster Works in September 1935 (as No 2509), shuts off at the sighting of a caution signal while climbing up to High Dyke and Stoke Tunnel from Grantham. The locomotive was allocated to Kings Cross (34A). *8th August 1959*

Great Ponton

Right: This locomotive was one of the original twelve Great Northern Railway class A1 3-cylinder 4-6-2's designed by H N Gresley. Built at Doncaster Works in April 1923 as No 1475 *Flying Fox*, it was eventually withdrawn in December 1964 as BR No 60106. Ultimately, these original A1s (not to be confused with the Thompson and Peppercorn A1 class locomotives of the 1940s) were all converted to A3s. The third road to the right of the picture was an up goods line which ran from Grantham up to High Dyke just short of Stoke Tunnel, which allowed goods trains to proceed south of Grantham without impeding the Kings Cross bound expresses on the climb up to Stoke Summit. *8th August 1959*

Nottingham Victoria Station

Above: Former LNER 2-6-0 K3 class No 61866, allocated to Immingham (40B) Motive Power Depot and fitted with the Automatic Warning System, stands on the up goods heading a train of fish vans.

Nottingham Victoria station opened in May 1900 and was closed to passengers in September 1967. Through goods working ceasing in May 1968. To the right of the locomotive is a fogman's hut, a once familier sight on the railways. The equipment in front of the hut was designed to allow the

fogman to lay the detonators on adjoining tracks, without endangering his safety by having to cross them. This site was redeveloped as the Victoria shopping precinct and only the original station clock tower has survived to remind us of scenes like this. *8th August 1959*

Hednesford – Cannock Wood Branch

Left: The National Coal Board's No.2 Area (Cannock Chase) afternoon miners' train runs down to Hednesford, headed by No 5 *Beaudesert,* a Fox Walker built 0-6-0ST of 1875, works number 266. Fox Walker & Co was taken over by Peckett & Sons Ltd in 1880. The coach, formerly LNWR No 22687, was a brake-third, built at Wolverton Works in 1917. *14th August 1959*

Wadebridge Station

Beattie 2-4-0WT No 30567 draws a GWR 'Toad' brake van and two wagons off the rear of a Bodmin Road mixed train. Being only 12½ ton axle loading and 12½ft wheelbase, three were retained at Wadebridge to work the lightly laid china clay branch to Wenford Bridge. *24th August 1959*

Wadebridge Station

Top: Dugald Drummond's T9 class 4-4-0s, known as 'Greyhounds' were built between 1899 and 1901 for the London & South Western Railway, fitted with 8-wheeled tenders and stove-pipe chimneys. Pictured here are No 30338 waiting to depart with a Padstow train and No 30715 arriving with the 12.58pm Padstow to Oakhampton service. No 30120 is preserved as part of the National Collection and at present is located on the Swanage Railway. *24th August 1959*

Halwill Junction Station

Above: Maunsell designed the N class 2-6-0 locomotives for the South Eastern & Chatham Railway, where they were introduced in 1917. A further batch was built in 1925 when the Southern Railway purchased 50 full sets of parts made at Woolwhich Arsenal under a government sponsored scheme to give munitions workers employment in peace time. Here No 31836 hauls the 12.58pm Padstow to London Waterloo service. *24th August 1959*

Bodmin General Station

Top: The GWR 4500 class 2-6-2T was introduced by G J Churchward in 1906. No 5539, pictured here, was an example of a further development, known as the 4575 class. It has arrived with the 10.10am Bodmin Road to Wadebridge local service. The engine will run round its train using the crossover in the foreground, before proceeding on its journey. This locomotive is preserved on the Butetown Historic Railway Society at Cardiff. *24th August 1959*

Barnstaple Junction

Above: No 30033, seen arriving with a local service from Bideford, is a former London & South Western Railway M7 class 0-4-4T introduced in 1897. The line off to the right leads to Ilfracombe. *25th August 1959*

Iron Bridge and Broseley Station

Top: An unidentified 4300 class 2-6-0 proceeds towards Buildwas with a 'Toad' brake van on the now closed section of the Severn Valley line, between Sutton Bridge Junction in Shrewsbury and Bridgnorth.
19th September 1959

Coalport LNWR Station

Lower left: A Western Region 3-car cross-country set, introduced in 1957, is utilised for an SLS railtour. The 8¼ mile line from Hadley Junction opened in June 1861, but it lost its passenger services in June 1952 and was completely closed in July 1964.
12th September 1959

Birmingham New Street Station

Lower right: Long before the days of visual display units, finger clocks were a common means of indicating to passengers the next train from each platform. The sign points to the 13.46 to Gt Yarmouth via the M&GNR. Note the 'Pines Express' boards (northbound) in the rack. *28th February 1959*

Bath S&D Joint MPD

In 1914 Derby Works commenced building six 2-8-0s for operating the hilly Somerset & Dorset Joint line; they were numbered 80-85. An additional five were purchased from Robert Stephenson & Company of Darlington in 1925 and numbered 86-90. All eleven were absorbed into LMS stock in 1930 and numbered 9670-9680. In 1932 they were renumbered 13800-13810 and in 1948, under BR, they became 53800-53810. The locomotive pictured here, No 53809, was withdrawn in June 1964 and sent to Barry for scrapping. It was removed in December 1975 and is now returned to full working order and is part of the Midland Railway Centre stock at Butterley. No 53808 is also preserved and currently resides at Minehead on the West Somerset Railway.
26th August 1959

Stourbridge Junction Station

Left centre: The GWR 6100 class 2-6-2Ts were usually associated with suburban services in the London area. This example, No 6111, carries green lined livery and may well be running-in following overhaul at Wolverhampton Works. It is standing in No 4 platform with a train for Wolverhampton Low Level via Dudley, a line which remains open for goods traffic as far as Round Oak.
9th October 1959

Retford Station

Above: A rare cast iron weight restriction notice. The Manchester, Sheffield & Lincolnshire Railway Company changed its name to the Great Central Railway in 1897.
4th October 1959

Staveley Motive Power Depot (38D)

Left: Great Central Railway, J. G. Robinson class D11 4-4-0 No 62663 *Prince Albert*, built at Gorton Works in 1920, one of a class of 35 locomotives, in open storage. At this time it was still quite safe to store locomotives away from the main shed area and find the name, number and shed plates (41H in this instance) untouched by souvenir hunters.
4th October 1959

Staveley Motive Power Depot

Stored out of use is former Midland Railway Deeley-designed 0-4-0T No 41531, used on the sharp radius siding curves around the steel works and collieries of South Yorkshire. A small class of ten, Nos 1528 to 1532 built at Derby Works in 1907 and Nos 1533 to 1537 built in 1921/2. Numbers 41528 and 41533 survived until 1966. *4th October 1959*

Metropolitan Cammell Saltley Works

Centre left: The *Midland Pullman*, comprising car numbers 60092/3, 60732/3 and 60742/3, completed and ready for testing. This, regarded by many as the fore-runner of the HST, was introduced into service on 4th July 1960 when it formed the 08.50 from Manchester Central to London St Pancras, taking 3¼ hrs for the journey. The return working left St Pancras at 18.10. An intermediate service to Leicester was run at 12.45, returning at 14.33, due at St Pancras at 16.00 hrs. It was later transferred to the Western Region where it was eventually withdrawn in 1973. *22nd October 1959*

Banbury Merton Street Station

Centre right and bottom right: The 21-mile branch from Banbury to Verney Junction, opened in May 1850, was due to close, as far as Buckingham, in January 1960, but difficulties in setting up a bus service to replace the trains extended its life until January 1961. The rest of the line from Buckingham to Verney Junction closed to passengers in September 1964 and to goods in December 1966. The track was lifted in 1967. Waiting in the somewhat dilapidated surroundings to work the 10.50 local service to Bletchley, is the Derby-built Motor Brake Second single unit railcar No 79900, Lot No 30380 of 1956. It was withdrawn in October 1967 and transferred to the Derby Research Department, where it became Test Car *'Iris'* (internal user No 975010). The railcar was rescued for preservation in 1995. *12th December 1959*

Lichfield Trent Valley Junction

Left: S W Johnson-designed former Midland Railway 0-6-0 No 43340, built at Derby works in the early 1890s, powers a through Horninglow (Burton-on-Trent) to Bescot goods. The locomotive was allocated to Burton (17B) MPD. *6th February 1960*

Crewe South MPD

Centre left: Stanier designed LMSR 2-6-0 No 42955 was built at Crewe in December 1933 and withdrawn April 1966. Locomotive No 42968 from this class is preserved on the Severn Valley Railway. *7th February 1960*

Colwich Junction – 127¼ mp WCML

Bottom left: A view of the station, signal box and Station Master's house. The station opened in December 1847, was closed in February 1958 and totally removed by June 1960. The LNWR signal box closed on 28th May 1961, being replaced by a BR (LM Region) design 130 yards further south on the up side. The house remains. The junction layout was completely remodelled in 1961. Multiple aspect signalling was introduced between Colwich and Stafford No 5 in May 1962, Colwich and Lichfield Trent Valley in July 1962 and on to Macclesfield in 1966. The overhead line equipment was energised between Stafford and Lichfield Trent Valley in August 1963 and from Colwich to Macclesfield in October 1966. A collision took place at Colwich Junction on 19th September 1986, the diamond crossing being the point of impact, although on a layout revised since this picture was taken. The trains involved were the 17.00 London Euston to Manchester Piccadilly and 17.20 Liverpool Lime Street to London Euston. Both the electric locomotives involved, 86.429 *The Times* and 86.211 *City of Milton Keynes*, were subsequently scrapped. The 900 or so passengers being carried in the two expresses suffered no fatalities, though tragically the driver of the Liverpool to London train lost his life.
21st February 1960

Hademore Troughs – 113½ mp WCML

Opposite page top: English Electric type 4 D235 pilots the down 'Red Rose' express. The steam heating boiler has failed and to keep passengers warm, former LMS class 5MT No 44711, built at Horwich works in 1948, has been attached at Rugby Midland. D235, a 2000 hp diesel-electric 1 Co-Co 1, was built at the Vulcan Foundry in October 1959, named *Apapa* in May 1962, renumbered 40.035 in March 1974 and was destined to be cut up in June 1985. The down line trough was removed on 4th December 1960. *27th February 1960*

Hademore Troughs – 113½ mp WCML

Below: Stanier 4-6-2 No 46226 *Duchess of Norfolk* passes over the down trough with the 'Mid-day Scot'. The LMR had a total of 35 water troughs, the average length being around 500yds; Hademore was the longest at over 640yds. Twenty-eight sets had their own water softening plants installed alongside to remove impurities, chiefly limescale, harmful to the locomotive boilers, from the water pumped into the troughs. Only the Southern Railway had no need to provide troughs to replenish locomotives when running, due to the shorter distances between stops. 46226 was built at Crewe Works in May 1938 as a steamlined locomotive; the casing being removed in June 1947. After a lifetime of service on the WCML it was finally withdrawn in September 1964. *27th February 1960*

Stourport Power Station

Left: English Electric 4-wheel 2ft 6in gauge, Exide Ironclad battery locomotive No 1 was built at Preston in 1925 (works No 688). A similar locomotive, No 2, constructed in the same year (works No 689) was also used on this site.

Centre left: WA No 2, inscribed 'CEA Midlands Division', is a Peckett 0-4-0 saddle tank (works No 1893 of 1936). This engine formerly worked at Buildwas Power Station in Shropshire where it was given the registration number 182 by the GWR in 1937 as it had occasion to work over BR tracks, and was therefore required to be inspected and registered by a pre-nationalised company or by BR. This registration number was usually carried on a plate on the cabside, although no such plate is evident in this photograph. It was later renamed *Ironbridge No 2* and preserved at the Great Western Railway Museum, Coleford.

Bottom left: General Wade Hayes was a Bagnall 0-4-0ST (works No 2665) supplied new in 1942.

Bottom right: Barclay 0-4-0ST *Sir Thomas Royden*, (works No 2088 of 1940) was also supplied new and is now preserved at the Rutland Railway Museum, Cottesmore.

All photographs taken on 5th March 1960

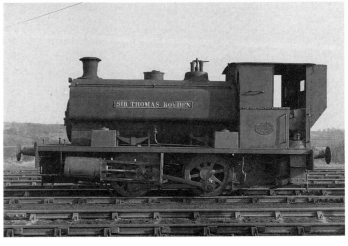

Round Oak Steel Works

Right: *Princess Margaret* was an 0-4-0ST built by Andrew Barclay, (works No 2115 of 1941). She was scrapped in November 1963 when steam operation gave way to diesel, but that in turn ended with closure of the works in December 1982. This site, in the heart of the Black Country, has since been developed into the Merry Hill shopping centre. *5th March 1960*

Rawnsley Shed, Cannock Chase

Centre right: The Lilleshall Company at St Georges, Oakengates, in Shropshire, was established in 1764 and in the 1890s was building locomotives. 0-6-0ST No 2 *Anglesey* was one of their products, completed in 1868.

Bottom right: *Anglesey* worked alongside sister locomotive No 1 *Marquis*, which had been built at Oakengates in 1867. Another Lilleshall locomotive, NCB 0-6-0ST No 4 *Rawnsley,* was originally built as a 2-2-2 in 1867 for the Paris exhibition, but was converted to 0-6-0 in 1872 and sold to Cannock & Rugeley Colliery Co Ltd.

Both photographs taken on 6th March 1960

Littleton Colliery

Below: This colliery, sunk at the turn of the century, was connected to the LNWR Wolverhampton to Stafford line at Penkridge by a 4 mile long branch line. All the locomotives owned by The Littleton Collieries Ltd were built by Manning Wardle. 0-6-0ST *Littleton No 2* was works No 1596, built in 1903. This pit, the last in the Cannock Chase Coalfield, closed in December 1993.
6th March 1960

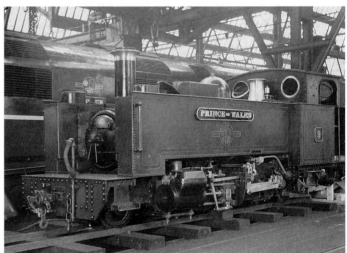

Lichfield Trent Valley Junction

Top: Ex-LMS class 4F 0-6-0 No 44599 takes a ballast train destined for Rugeley, down the connecting branch between the high and low level junctions. Note the non-standard tender and the former LMS designed 'plough' ballast brake van. *19th March 1960*

Banbury MPD (84C)

Centre left: Ex-GWR No 7206, one of 54 2-8-0Ts rebuilt into 2-8-2Ts by C B Collett between 1934 and 1939 in order to increase bunker capacity to 6 tons and water to 2500 gallons. *20th March 1960*

Swindon Works

Centre right: Vale of Rheidol Railway 2-6-2T (1ft 11½in gauge) No 9 *Prince of Wales* on general overhaul. It was built by Davies & Metcalfe of Romiley in 1902 and operates the line today with two similar locomotives built by the GWR in 1923. *20th March 1960*

Milford and Brocton – 129½ mp WCML

Right: Former LMS 'Jubilee' No 45704 *Leviathan*, built at Crewe Works in 1936 and withdrawn in January 1965, heads the 09.10 Llandudno to London Euston express, past the site once occupied by a station which opened May 1877 and closed March 1950. New works have commenced to provide two additional tracks, going behind the existing signal box, to extend the 4-track section south beyond Tixall Road bridge, which had replaced the original level crossing in 1877. New up and down fast lines were built and upon completion the four tracks to Stafford were transposed on 29th/30th May 1960 to read, from left to right – down slow, up slow, down fast and up fast – which conformed to the running north of Stafford. *26th March 1960*

Colwich – 126½ mp WCML

Above: Overbridge No 129 in the course of being raised to accommodate the overhead electric catenery. The brick-built part of the bridge on the left over the down lines dates from the opening of the line in the 1840s. The girder section over the up lines was a result of quadrupling Colwich to Armitage at the beginning of the century. *26th March 1960*

Shugborough – 128¾ mp WCML

Above: Aquaduct bridge No 140 and overbridge No 141. The preparatory work to allow for overhead electrification on this stretch of the line involved the construction of a concrete arch. The track sections are made up of 109 lb rail in 60ft lengths on wooden sleepers. The down distant signal post for Milford and Brocton has black/white horizontal background bands to aid identification. *2nd April 1960*

Shugborough – 128½ mp WCML

Right: Underbridge No.139, south of Shugborough tunnel, was built with this fine stonework embellishment as befitting at the entrance to Shugborough Hall. Former LMS 'Royal Scot' class No 46144 *Honourable Artillery Company*, originally named *Ostrich*, travels south with the 10.00 Blackpool Central to London Euston express. *2nd April 1960*

Bicester Central Ordnance Depot

Opposite page bottom: Ministry of Supply 0-6-0ST No WD132 *Sapper* was built by Hunslet at Leeds in 1944, (works No 3163). The locomotive was registered to work over BR lines and carried Railway Executive plate No 427/52. At the time of writing the loco is preserved on the South Devon Railway and bore the name *Joseph* until recommissioned at Buckfastleigh on 17th June 1995 as No 132 *Sapper*. *20th March 1960*

Stafford Station

Top left: The frontage before demolition started in September 1960 and rebuilding commenced. The station was opened in July 1837 by the Grand Junction Railway. *2nd April 1960*

Stafford No 5 Signal Box – 134 mp

Centre left: The view from bridge No 85 overlooking No 5 Signal box, which contained a 150-lever frame made in Crewe in 1952 and still in use today. The loco yard, with its mechanical coaling plant, No 6 Signal Box and the station can also be seen. Ex-LMS 'Patriot' class No 45537 *Private E. Sykes V.C.* stands in the down platform with the 09.10 Birmingham New Street to Liverpool and Manchester. *2nd April 1960*

Stafford (Trent Valley Junc) – 133 mp

Below: About half a mile south of the station was Stafford Trent Valley Junction. The tracks heading off to the right of the signal box are those of the Grand Junction Line leading to Bushbury Junction near Wolverhampton which opened in July 1837. At the time this picture was taken the three tracks along the GJR to Rickerscote were the up loop, up and down lines. These were changed when the line was electrified in 1962 to up, up loop and down lines. The five tracks on the Trent Valley route to the left of the signal box were through up siding to Queensville, up slow, up fast, down fast and down slow. These were transposed in May 1960 to read: up siding, up fast, down fast, up slow, down slow, to conform with the pattern of the tracks between Stafford and Crewe. The line from Stafford south to Milford and Brockton had originally been quadrupled in 1898. No 1 Signal Box (seen here) closed in 1962. *2nd April 1960*

Stafford Station, South end

Top: A view taken from bridge No 84, Newport Road, prior to roof and building demolition which commenced in May 1960. Multiple aspect signalling replaced the semaphores in May 1962 and the overhead line equipment was switched on through the station area in November 1962. A group of youthful trainspotters are sitting on the site of the former cattle dock awaiting developments on the adjacent tracks. The 3-coach corridor set in the station will later form a service calling at all stations to Wellington and Shrewsbury. *2nd April 1960*

Queensville – 132½mp WCML

Above: A view looking north as 'The Merseyside Express' behind English Electric type 4 No D222 (later 40 022) passes through on the up fast line. The up siding from Stafford No 1, which served the English Electric factory in the distance, joins the up slow outside the box. The sidings to the left of the picture, and the associated diamond crossovers in the foreground, served the British Reinforced Concrete Works. With the introduction of multiple aspect signalling, Queensville box became a shunt frame to allow access to these sidings. When rail traffic from these ceased, the box was demolished in July 1977. *2nd April 1960*

Stafford No 5 Junctions – 134¼ mp

Top: English Electric type 4 diesel No D218 (later 40 018) on the up fast line with the 'Shamrock Express' from the Crewe direction. The tracks curving round to the left by W G Bagnall's Castle Works were those of the Shropshire Union line to Wellington, opened in June 1849 and closed in August 1966, except for the section between Wellington and Newport. The lines to the right are those of the former GNR branch to Bromshall Junction which opened in December 1867 and closed in March 1957 except for a short section to Stafford Common retained to serve a RAF MU depot. *2nd April 1960*

Rugeley Trent Valley Station – 124¼ mp WCML

Above: Former LMS 2-8-0 No 48188 passes through on the up fast line with a lengthy goods. The locomotive was built in April 1942 by the North British Locomotive Company at Glasgow and withdrawn in May 1966. Note that track circuits were not in situ, as denoted by the 'D' signs fixed to each signal post indicating to drivers that being held at any of these signals necessitated the fireman alighting and pressing the plungers provided at the trackside to remind the signalman at Rugeley No 1 Signal Box of their presence. No 2 Signal Box can be seen behind the train beyond the footbridge. *2nd April 1960*

Colwich – 127¼ mp WCML

Above: Former LMS 4-6-2 No 46243 *City of Lancaster* passes under bridge No 130 with the 11.20 London Euston to Manchester London Road. The train is travelling on the down fast line which was transposed in December 1961 to become the down slow. Note the down lines pass under the original brick arch, the up lines pass under the steel girder construction. This was a result of quadrupling of tracks between Colwich and Armitage at the turn of the century. *2nd April 1960*

Baswich – 131mp WCML

Centre right: Former LNWR 0-8-0 No 49081 heads a long goods train on the up slow line. The slow line at this location was upgraded and became the up fast in May 1962, upon completion of remodelling and new track layout at Milford & Brocton. This coincided with the introduction of multiple aspect signalling (MAS) operation. Overhead line equipment (OLE) was energised in August 1963. *2nd April 1960*

Rugeley Trent Valley No 1 Signal Box

Right: The up 'Royal Scot' passes No 1 Signal Box behind 'Coronation' class No 46240 *City of Coventry*. The tracks to the left are to Ryecroft Junction, Walsall. MAS was introduced in July 1962, and the OLE energised through here in August 1963. No 1 Signal Box closed in October 1974 together with the junction connection; a ladder junction introduced north of Rugeley now serves the branch. Note the old 'C' board beside the down slow, indicating the start of a temporary speed restriction. *2nd April 1960*

Polesworth Station – 106½ mp WCML

Opposite page, top: English Electric 2000 hp 1 Co-Co 1 diesel electric type 4 No D267 (later 40 067) works the 08.30 Carlisle and Windermere to London. D267 was built at Vulcan Foundry in March 1960, withdrawn on 7th July 1981 and cut up in April 1982. The station was unstaffed from October 1972 and the Livock-designed buildings were demolished. The signal box closed in July 1990 and was also removed *9th April 1960*

Atherstone Station – 102 mp WCML

Opposite page, bottom: The station has been unstaffed since 1972. The original 1840s J W Livock-designed Grade 2 listed station buildings on the up side were renovated in the 1980s by the private owners who bought them from BR. The signal box above the down and up fast lines (with its own access footbridge) was closed in November 1962 and replaced by one of BR (LMR) design, in the down sidings, but this too was closed in July 1970 and subsequently demolished. A further 120 yds south, the quadrupling of tracks between Tamworth and Atherstone was completed in 1901. *9th April 1960*

Photographs on this page:

Tamworth – 110 mp WCML

Top right: 'The Mid-Day Scot', the 13.30 London Euston to Glasgow Central, heads north behind former LMS 'Coronation' class 4-6-2 No 46254 *City of Stoke on Trent*, built at Crewe in September 1946, withdrawn in September 1964 and scrapped at Cashmores at Great Bridge in 1965 *9th April 1960*

Ashby Junction – 98 mp WCML

Centre right: The signal box closed with the extension of MAS through to Brinklow in October 1963. The tracks to the right are to Weddington Junction and Shackerstone junction, both closed in 1963. The overbridge, to the north, carried the Abbey Junction to Weddington Junction connection, closed in 1964 after a period when it was used for wagon storage. *9th April 1960*

Baddesley Sidings – 102¾ mp WCML

Right: A view from overbridge No 65, looking south at the Trent Valley line outlet for Baddesley Colliery coal trains. These were often worked by the NCB's Garratt locomotive (see page 77) which gained access via the busy A5 ungated road crossing. The signal box closed on 10th/11th November 1962 due to the introduction of multiple aspect signalling between Lichfield Trent Valley and Ashby Junction. While the colliery remained working, coal was despatched by the Midland Railway branch to Kingsbury Sidings. Note the original crossing keeper's cottage in the right foreground. *9th April 1960*

Ashby Junction – 98 mp WCML

Left: Ex-LMS Pacific locomotive No 46203 *Princess Margaret Rose* works the 07.55 London Euston to Liverpool. Built at Crewe in July 1935, this locomotive ran until October 1962. Following withdrawal it went to Butlin's Pwllheli holiday camp as a static exhibit. Under a 'free loan with an option to purchase' arrangement it was moved to Derby Works on 11th May 1975, and then onto the Midland Railway Centre at Butterley on 4/5th November of that same year, where it languished for around 13 years until eventually passing into private ownership. Restoration to full main line working standard commenced. It was first steamed on 8th May 1990, did test-runs on BR metals on 15/17th May and made its first revenue run on 2nd June 1990, around the Derby-Sheffield circular route. It has since gone on to make many main line appearances.
9th April 1960

Wellingborough

Centre left: The late-running overnight Edinburgh and Leeds to London St Pancras sleeper express behind 'Jubilee' class 4-6-0s Nos 45570 *New Zealand* and 45576 *Bombay*. Note the two glass-lined 6-wheeled milk tanks next to the locomotives.
10th April 1960

Cambridge Motive Power Depot (31A)

Bottom left: Great Eastern Railway 0-6-0 J17 Class No 65554 designed by J Holden and rebuilt at Stratford in 1928. *10th April 1960*

March Motive Power Depot (31B)

Opposite page, top: Ex-LNER O1 class No 63890, built in 1919 and rebuilt under Edward Thompson in 1946. *10th April 1960*

New England MPD, Peterborough (35A)

Opposite page centre: Ex-LNER 0-6-2T N2/4 69582, built by Hawthorn Leslie & Company of Newcastle, (works No 3705 of 1929) stands alongside V2 class 2-6-2 No 60902, built at Darlington in 1940. The N2/4 is fitted with condensing apparatus and a small chimney for working over electrified lines in the London area. *10th April 1960*

Hademore Troughs – 113½ mp WCML

Bottom right: 'Coronation' class 4-6-2 No 46242 *City of Glasgow*, is working the up 'Royal Scot'. Built at Crewe Works in 1940 as a streamliner, its casing was removed in March 1947 and it was eventually withdrawn in October 1963. The absence of ballast where water troughs were laid is noticeable as water spillage would wash the ballast away and weaken the formation, therefore concrete slabs were interlaced with the sleepers and were also used to line the cesses. Any spillage would run into the drainage channels on either side of the formation *23rd April 1960*

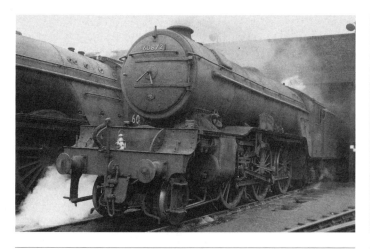

Old Oak Common (81A) MPD

Opposite page top: The 1500 class was a late development in the long line of 0-6-0 pannier tanks which had been introduced by the GWR over many decades. Designed by F W Hawksworth, the GWR's last Chief Mechanical Engineer, the ten locomotives which made up the class were in fact built under the auspices of BR in 1949. Class leader No 1500 displays the wartime utility aspects of her design, notably the absence of a running plate. The only class survivor is No 1501, on the Severn Valley Railway. *1st May 1960*

Opposite page bottom: GWR Churchward designed 2-8-0 No 4701, built in 1922, was one of a small class of nine introduced to work fast fitted freight trains to the west of England and Birkenhead from the London area. Heavy machines, classified as mixed traffic locomotives, with 'Red' route restriction, they were often called upon to work passenger trains. *1st May 1960*

This page, top right: No 9702 represents a variation to the GWR 5700 class first introduced by C B Collett in 1929. It was one of 11 locomotives, numbered 9700 to 9710, that were introduced in 1933, fitted with Weir feed pumps and condensing apparatus, for working over the Metropolitan lines. *1st May 1960*

Kings Cross MPD (34A) ECML

This page, above left: This country's first 3-cylinder 2-6-2 locomotives were introduced in 1936 by H N Gresley on the LNER and designated as the V2 class. Pictured here, carrying a 36A (Doncaster) shed code plate, is No 60872 *Kings Own Yorkshire Light Infantry* – a name later transferred to 'Deltic' D9002. No 60872 was built at Doncaster in 1939. *1st May 1960*

Willesden MPD (1A) WCML

This page, below: These Fowler designed 2-6-2Ts were built at Derby and introduced by the LMSR in 1930. The class of 70 locomotives originally carried the numbers 15500 to 15569 but were renumbered 1 to 70 in 1934 and then again from 40001 to 40070 by BR in 1948. Built for suburban services such as St. Pancras to Bedford, they were considered poor machines, constantly losing time between stations, mainly due to their small boilers being unable to provide sufficient steam. When constructed they were provided with inside steam pipes, later placed outside. Pictured here are Nos 40003 and 40051. *1st May 1960*

Neasden MPD, London (34E)

Opposite page, top: British Railways acquired a total of 645 2-6-4Ts. Some, designed by Fowler, dated back to 1927; others were by Stanier (from 1934) and by Fairburn (from 1945). Two hundred and fifty of the Fairburn design, numbered 42050 to 42299 and 42673 to 42699, were built in a series of small batches, the majority at Derby between 1945 and 1951, but Brighton Works produced 41, (42066 to 42106) in 1950-51, when under BR ownership. Seen here are Nos 42230, built in June 1946 and withdrawn in August 1965, and No 42091, built in April 1951 and withdrawn in October 1963. *1st May 1960*

Hatfield MPD (34C)

Top: Large numbers of these 0-6-2Ts were used by the LNER for the frequent suburban services out of its London terminus and were thus inherited by BR. Pictured here is N7/3 class 0-6-2T No 69696 built by W Beardmore & Company in 1927 as an N7/2 No 2656 (works No 319). Renumbered 69696, it was fitted with a round-topped fire box in 1946, and with push-pull apparatus in 1951. Withdrawal came in April 1961. *1st May 1960*

Stratford MPD, London (30A)

Above: The former LNER J15 class 0-6-0 No 65476 was originally one of the Y14 class designed by T W Worsdell for the Great Eastern Railway and introduced in 1883. Two hundred and ninety had been constructed between the introduction of the class and 1913 when the last one was built. *1st May 1960*

Hornsey (34B) MPD

Opposite page, bottom: The former LNER J50 class 0-6-0Ts were originally designed for freight and shunting duties for the GNR by H N Gresley in 1922 and 102 were eventually built between 1922 and 1937. Standing outside the shed are Nos 68936, a J50/2 of 1922; 68986, 68987 – a pair of J50/4s with larger bunker, introduced in 1937; and 68896, a J50/1, rebuilt from the smaller J51 of 1913-14 and introduced into service in 1929 . *1st May 1960*

Irchester Ironstone Quarries

Left: Rothwell, a Peckett-built 0-4-0ST (works No 1258 of 1912) and *Progress,* also an 0-6-0ST by Peckett of Bristol (works No 1402 of 1915), stand awaiting their fate at the South Durham Steel & Iron Co Ltd's workings near Wellingborough. They had some time to wait, for it was not until December 1966 that they both went to Cohen's at Cransley, for scrap.
14th May 1960

Wellingborough Ironworks

Centre left: Wellingborough Iron Co Ltd's 0-4-0ST locomotive *Wellingborough No.6* was built by Hudswell Clarke & Rodgers in 1876 and rebuilt in 1920. It is seen here out of use and was cut up in the following April. The Ironworks themselves closed in October 1962. *14th May 1960*

Armitage Station – 121 mp WCML

Below: On the day the station closed *The Shamrock* express passes through the up platform headed by D234 (later 40.034), a type 4 2000hp 1Co-Co1 built by English Electric at the Vulcan Foundry in October 1959. It was named *Accra* in May 1962, withdrawn in January 1984 and cut-up at Doncaster in April 1984. *11th June 1960*

Armitage Station – 121 mp WCML

Below: Another view taken on the day the station closed. 'Jubilee' class 4-6-0 No 45633 *Aden,* which carried the name *Trans-Jordan* until 1946, is seen on the down line. The station footbridge was removed the following day, the buildings and platforms were demolished in the autumn of 1960. Note the sack barrow on the up platform. *11th June 1960*

Rolleston-on-Dove (Burton-Tutbury)

Above: This was the final day before withdrawal of passenger services on this 5½ mile North Staffs Railway branch which opened in September 1848. The service from Burton-on-Trent to Tutbury was operated by push-pull sets. Known locally as the 'Tutbury Jenny', here the 16.37 to Burton is being propelled through the station, which closed in the 1940s, by LMS 2-6-2T No 41277. *11th June 1960*

Stretton and Clay Mills Station

Above: The 'Tutbury Jenny' with 2-6-2T No 41277 in charge of the push-pull set forming the 16.12 Burton-on-Trent to Tubury on the final day of the service, passes through Stretton and Clay Mills Station which closed on 1st January 1949. Although the station has been closed for 11 years, it is intact and unmolested by vandals or souvenir hunters. Railway memorabilia was not sought after in those days. That station nameboard would have disappeared upon closure today. The line was opened in September 1848 by the North Staffordshire Railway and closed in stages between 1966 and 1968.
11th June 1960

Hademore Troughs – 113½ mp WCML

Bottom left: The lightly loaded afternoon local down pick-up freight from Tamworth to Stafford takes water behind H G Ivatt designed LMSR 2-6-0 No 43034, built at the old Lancashire & Yorkshire works at Horwich in May 1949 and withdrawn in May 1967.
18th June 1960

Farnborough Station – 33¼ mp

Right: Rebuilt 'Merchant Navy' class 4-6-2 No 35011 *General Steam Navigation* hurries through with an up Bournemouth Central to London Waterloo express. Built in 1944 and rebuilt in 1959, it was withdrawn in February 1966, but fortunately was one of the many Bulleid Pacifics to be rescued from the Woodhams' scrapyard at Barry in South Wales. In recent years it has been stored on a open siding at Brighton, in ex-Barry condition. Note the LSWR low pressure pneumatic power operated lower quadrant arms on this delightful gantry.
26th June 1960

Fleet – 37½ mp (from Waterloo)

Below: No 30514, pictured here travelling the down slow line with a London Waterloo to Salisbury train, was the penultimate example of the first batch of the 4-6-0 S15 class mixed traffic locomotives designed by R W Urie for the London & South Western Railway, and introduced in 1920.
2nd July 1960

Fleet – 37½ mp

Left: The 'Battle of Britain' class 4-6-2 was introduced in 1945 to O V Bulleid's design for a smaller version of the 'Merchant Navy' class, capable of working almost anywhere. Rebuilt locomotive No 34050 *Royal Observer Corps* is seen here with a down express near Fleet. *2nd July 1960*

Fleet Station – 36½ mp

Centre left: In 1926 R E L Maunsell introduced his 'Lord Nelson' class 4-6-0 locomotive, a 4-cylinder design. Sixteen were built, of which No 30865 *Sir John Hawkins* was the last. O V Bulleid had the task of rebuilding the class into more successful performers. No 850 *Lord Nelson* has been preserved and is resident at Steamtown, Carnforth. *2nd July 1960*

Below: In 1925 R E L Maunsell added to R W Urie's 1918 design of N15 class 2-cylinder 4-6-0 locomotives by placing an order for 30 (Nos 793 to 806) with the North British Locomotive Company in Glasgow. They were named after Knights of the Round Table and known as the 'King Arthur' class. Pictured here is No 30773 *Sir Lavaine*, passing through on the up fast with a London Waterloo express. *2nd July 1960*

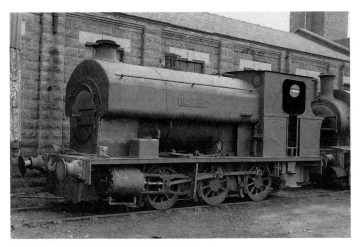 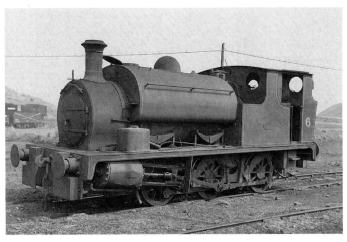

 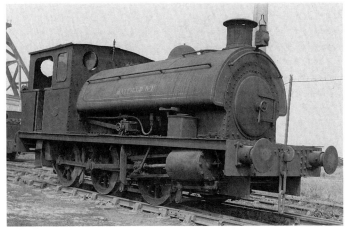

Markham Main Colliery, South Yorkshire

Top left: At this pit near Doncaster was *Herbert*, an 0-6-0ST by Avonside Engine Co. (works number 1950 of 1924). It was scrapped about 1963. *3rd July 1960*

Rossington Main Colliery, South Yorkshire

Centre left: This pit was also in the Doncaster area. Hudswell Clarke 0-6-0ST *Irene* was built in 1903, (works number 655) and was scrapped during 1961. *3rd July 1960*

Desborough Ironstone Quarries (Sheepbridge Co Ltd)

Bottom left: Known as No 3, this 0-6-0ST is of uncertain identity, but it was possibly built in 1883 by Black Hawthorn, rebuilt in 1915 and 1935, and scrapped in February 1962. *3rd July 1960*

Hatfield Main Colliery, South Yorkshire

This was another of the many collieries in the Doncaster area.

Top right: No 6 an 0-6-0ST built by Hudswell Clarke (works number 1349 of 1918) and rebuilt by the Yorkshire Engine Company in 1946. It was scrapped in April 1965.

Centre right: Inside cylinder 0-6-0ST *Hatfield No 3,* built by Kitson, (works number 3819 of 1899) was formerly Taff Vale Railway No 91, and Great Western No 791. It was scrapped in March 1963

Bottom right: Hatfield No 1, an 0-6-0ST built by Hawthorn Leslie (works no 3197 of 1916) and scrapped in April 1969.

All three photographs were taken on 3rd July 1960

Muskham Troughs, Newark – 121½ mp

Centre right: LNER A4 class 4-6-2 No 4496 *Golden Shuttle*, was built at Doncaster in September 1937. Renumbered 8 and renamed *Dwight D. Eisenhower* in September 1945, it became BR No 60008 in 1948 and is here working an up Newcastle to Kings Cross express on the East Coast main line. Withdrawn from service in July 1963, the A4 was shipped to the National Railroad Museum of America at Green Bay, Wisconsin in 1964. *23rd July 1960*

Bottom right: Former LNER V2 class 2-6-2 No 60809 *The Snapper, The East Yorkshire Regiment, the Duke of York's Own* with the 10.12 Grantham to Doncaster semi-fast. A triple articulated suburban set forms the first portion of the train. *23rd July 1960*

Sonning Cutting, near Twyford, GWML

Above: Ex-GWR 'King' class 4-6-0 No 6018 *King Henry VI* with a Plymouth to London Paddington express. Introduced in 1927, only 30 were built, as due to their 22½ ton axle load they were restricted to the London to Plymouth and London to Wolverhampton via Bicester routes. Three examples of the class are preserved *16th July 1960*

Sonning Cutting, near Twyford, GWML

Opposite page top: The GWR 4-6-0 4073 4-cylinder 'Castle' class was introduced by Collett in 1923. No 5068 *Beverston Castle* was built at Swindon in June 1938 and withdrawn in September 1962. It is here on the down fast with a London Paddington to Weston-super-Mare train. *16th July 1960*

Opposite page bottom: 'Warship' class diesel-hydraulic Bo-Bo No D809 *Champion*, built at Swindon works in August 1959, was withdrawn in October 1971 and scrapped at Swindon a year later. It is seen here working a Kingswear and Paignton to London Paddington express. *16th July 1960*

East Coast Main Line – 121¼ mp

Above: A1 Pacific No 60130 *Kestrel*, built in September 1968 at Doncaster works, heads towards Muskham water troughs on the East Coast Main Line near Newark with a down Kings Cross to Newcastle express. The train has just crossed the River *Trent* on the girder bridge in the background. The locomotive carries the 56C shed plate of Copley Hill depot in Leeds. *23rd July 1960*

Lichfield Trent Valley (High Level)

Below: Gresley 3-cylinder K3 class 2-6-0 No 61865 works a Pleasley East to Dudley excursion. Although B1s were authorised to travel on this route K3s were not and this was probably the only occasion such a locomotive ventured onto this line. A3s did appear on the Stirling to Sutton Coldfield car sleeper service, but again were not authorised. *31st July 1960*

Muskham Troughs – 121¾ mp ECML

Above: Approach warning boards were to advise firemen that this was the point at which they should lower their scoop to pick up water. The LNER (GNR) style board has been supplemented by its BR equivalent in the form of the permanently lit Adlake oil lamp, displaying a white 'X' aspect. The ladder enabled the lampman to get up to fill and trim the lamp. *23rd July 1960*

Lichfield Trent Valley High Level

Above: During the '50s and early '60s, Bank Holiday excursions from the East Midlands to Dudley, for the zoo and castle, were very popular, often requiring all types of locomotives and stock to be pressed into service. Hughes-designed 2-6-0 No 42839, built at Horwich works in August 1930 and withdrawn June 1964, is working a half-day excursion from Trent. *31st July 1960*

Lichfield Trent Valley High Level Station

Right: Taking water on the down line is LMS-designed class 8F 2-8-0 No 48726, built at the SR's Brighton works in 1944 for the LNER. Originally numbered 7673, it became 3122 and then 3522 in the 1946 and 1947 renumberings. It was taken into LMS stock as No 8726 in 1947. 'Jubilee' class No 45654 *Hood* approaches with a diverted Newcastle to Bristol express. *14th August 1960*

Lichfield City

Above: The replacement of underbridge No 87 on the South Staffs line at Chesterfield Terrace called for the use of two cranes, both of 50 tons lifting capacity. Here, the Rugby (left) and Crewe North steam cranes lift the new down line deck section off the wagon on the up line. This part of the former South Staffordshire Railway between Ryecroft Junction and Anglesea sidings closed in January 1965. The section which remains, into Lichfield City, has been singled and is used by the twice weekly fuel oil train from Lindsey to Charrington's siding at Anglesea. *14th August 1960*

Waltham Ironstone Quarries

Above left: The Eastwell & Waltham Ironstone Company Limited operation at Melton Mowbray, Leics, was, unusually for Britain, a metre gauge system. The locomotive *Cambrai* was a 0-6-0T built by Corpet Louvet et Cie in 1888, La Courneuve works number 493. It had previously worked on the Chemin de Fer du Cambresis, in France. It was purchased by Loddington Ironstone Company in 1936 and remained at Waltham Ironstone Quarries from 1956 until the system closed in 1958. The locomotive is now preserved at the Irchester Narrow Gauge Museum. *28th August 1960*

Above: Metre gauge *Nantes*, also an 0-6-0T built by Vve L Corpet & L Louvet in Paris (works No 936 of 1903) came here in 1934 via T W Ward Ltd, from the Chemin de Fer de la Loire Inferieure, France. Although believed earmarked for preservation at one time, it was scrapped on site in December 1960. *28th August 1960*

Left: Manning Wardle 0-4-2ST *Dreadnought* (works No 1757) built in 1910, was also a metre gauge locomotive. It had been rebuilt in 1935 from 0-4-0ST and was scrapped at the same time as *Nantes*. *28th August 1960*

Eastwell Ironstone Quarries, Leics.

Below: A farewell trip to the Eastwell & Loddington Ironstone Co Ltd's 3ft gauge system, prior to closure, was organised by the Birmingham Locomotive Club. Members travelled in 20 tub wagons behind *Nancy*, an 0-6-0T built by the Avonside Engine Co in 1908 (works number 1547). The locomotive is now preserved on the Shanes Castle Railway in County Antrim in Northern Ireland. *28th August 1960*

Eastwell Ironstone Quarries, Leics.

Above: Five locos of the 3ft gauge system neatly placed for photography, these being *Underbank* an 0-4-0ST by Peckett (works No 873) of 1900, *Lord Granby* an 0-4-0ST by Hudswell Clarke (works No 633 of 1902), *Mountaineer* an 0-6-0ST by Bagnall (No 2203 of 1922), *Pioneer* an 0-6-0ST by Bagnall (No 1980) of 1913 and *Belvoir* an 0-6-0ST by Hunslet (No 1823) of 1936. All were scrapped in the next two years, except *Lord Granby*, which is preserved at the Leeds Industrial Museum, Armley Mills.

Below left: Underbank, a 0-4-0ST Peckett (works No 873 of 1900).

Centre right: The rope incline viewed from the winding house, looking down towards the railhead on the LNWR/GNR joint line between Stathern Junction and Scalford Junction. *Photographs taken 28th August 1960*

Sproxton Ironstone Quarries

Below right: Owned by the Park Gate Iron & Steel Co Ltd, *Hastings* was a 0-6-0ST built by the Hunslet Engine Company in Leeds (works number 469 of 1888). Following its withdrawal the locomotive found new ownership at Rolvenden on the Kent & East Sussex Railway. *28th August 1960*

Towyn Wharf

Opposite page top: No 4 *Edward Thompson* a Kerr Stuart 0-4-2ST built in 1921 (works number 4047) stands ready to depart for Abergynolwyn, in what was then a very bleak station area, on the 2ft 3in gauge Talyllyn railway. *31st August 1960*

This page top right: Russell, a 1ft 11½in gauge 2-6-2T Hunslet locomotive, was built in 1906, (works number 901) and had been cosmetically restored for display at the rear of the Talyllyn Museum at this time. By August 1977 it had returned to the line for which it had originally been built – The Welsh Highland Railway, at Portmadoc. *31st August 1960*

Portmadoc

Centre right: Double-ended 0-4-4-0T Fairlie patent locomotive No 10 *Merddin Emrys*, built at Boston Lodge Works in 1879, is ready to take another load of holiday passengers from the Harbour station to Tan-y-bwlch, running on a narrow gauge of 1ft 11½in. *30th August 1960*

Bottom right: '4500' class 2-6-2T No 5553, built by the GWR at Swindon in November 1928, was withdrawn in November 1961 and was sent to Woodham's yard at Barry for scrapping. It remained there until 1987 when Dai Woodham presented it to the Barry Development Partnership for preservation at a suitable location in the town. No 5553 is seen here working the up coast line portion of the 'Cambrian Express', 07.40 ex-Pwllheli to Dovey Junction, while '2251' class 0-6-0 No 2204 shunts the down side goods yard. *31st August 1960*

Dovey Junction

Opposite page bottom: A busy time at this isolated spot with the arrival of the 10.25 from Pwllheli, headed by BR Standard 2-6-0 No 78007, allocated to Machynlleth (89C), and the 12.40 Aberystwyth to Crewe express hauled by former GWR 4-6-0 No 7822 *Foxcote Manor*, allocated to Oswestry (89A). No 7822 was built at Swindon in December 1950 and is now preserved in full working order on the Llangollen Railway. No 78007 was built at Darlington in 1953, withdrawn in May 1967 and scrapped by A Draper at Hull. *31st August 1960*

Aberystwyth Station

Above: GWR Vale of Rheidol Railway No 7 *Owain Glyndwr*, a 2-6-2T built at Swindon in 1923 for the 11¾ mile 1ft 11½in gauge line opened in 1902, and sold to the Brecon Mountain Railway. *31st August 1960*

Snowdon Mountain Railway

Above right: Eight 0-4-2T rack locomotives were built by the Swiss Loco works in Winterthur between 1895 & 1923 to work the 4¾ mile, 800mm gauge line from Llanberis to the Summit. Pictured here propelling the usual single coach is No 6 *Padarn* (works number 2838 of 1922). *31st August 1960*

Chester General

Below: Former LMSR 3P 2-6-2T No 40202, built in 1938, departs with an express for Birkenhead Woodside via Hooton & Rock Ferry. The old LNWR No 3a signal box forms the backcloth while construction of a new No 3a was taking place behind the camera. This in turn was demolished when the Chester power box opened in 1984. The '6C' shed allocation plate of Birkenhead is carried on the smoke box. *31st August 1960*

Colwich – 126¹/₂ mp WCML

Above: Former LMSR 'Coronation' Class 8P
4-6-2 No 46252 *City of Leicester*, built at
Crewe Works in June 1944 and withdrawn
in May 1963, passes with a 14-coach relief to
the down 'Mid-day Scot'. The running of
extra trains of this size was not uncommon
at holiday times. *3rd September 1960*

Wimblebury Junction Signal Box

Centre right: In 1880 the LNWR authorised
constructed of the Littleworth Tramway
extension, to link up the line between
Cooper's Lodge Junction and Littleworth
Junction. The line trailing in here comes
from Cross Keys Junction, 1067 yards distant, leading forward to East Cannock
junction in 763 yards. The NCB were the
sole operators at this period, although the
site, signal box and level crossing were
owned by the 'Docks and Inland Waterways
Executive', as stated on the painted trespass
notice. The signal box had been freshly
repainted in green and cream colours.
3rd September 1960

Colwich – WCML 126¹/₂ mp

Bottom right: 'Princess Coronation' class 8P
4-6-2 No 46256 *Sir William A. Stanier, FRS*,
built at Crewe in December 1947 (at a cost
of £18,248) and withdrawn in October 1964,
hauls a 16-coach 'Mid-day Scot' on the down
fast. This line was transposed with the down
slow (right) between Armitage and Colwich
Junction on 17th December 1961.One of
46256's nameplates is displayed in Stanier
House, Birmingham. *3rd September 1960*

Gotham Sidings, near Nottingham

Left: An RCTS special, consisting of four brake-vans and five vacuum open wagons, is headed by former LMS 2-6-2T No 41280. This branch, which diverged in a westerly direction from Gotham Junction, situated north of Rushcliffe Halt and 2 miles south of Ruddington on the Great Central main line, led to the British Gypsum factory at Gotham. The present-day development of the former main line, north of Loughborough and as far as Ruddington, is being handled by Great Central Railway (Nottingham) Limited, who will oversee the construction of a new station and a locomotive and carriage shed, all in a traditional style, within the Nottingham Heritage Centre, on the site of the former Ruddington Ordnance Depot. Further south, in a reported £1million project designed to link the present Leicester-Loughborough section to Ruddington in the north, a 26 metre single span bridge will be reinstated over all four tracks of the Midland Main Line, just to the south of Loughborough Midland station. This project, which it is hoped will be completed in time for the line's centenary in 1999, will see this unique preserved main line railway extended to 18 miles in length. *10th September 1960*

Kingston-on-Soar Gypsum Mines

Centre left: Joining the Midland main line at Kegworth was the Gypsum Mines Ltd line on which a Railway Correspondence and Travel Society special was operated before the line's closure. The locomotive, named *Lady Angela*, is a 0-4-0ST, built by Peckett of Bristol in 1926 (works number 1690) and is now preserved on the South Devon Railway at Buckfastleigh. *10th September 1960*

Doncaster MPD

Left: No 90512, carrying a Frodingham 36C shed plate awaits its next turn of duty. More than 700 of these Riddles-designed Austerity 2-8-0s were built for the Ministry of Supply between 1943 and 1945, many seeing service on the railways of Europe before being repatriated to work on BR. *18th September 1960*

Doncaster Works

Above: General view of the erecting shop showing various locomotives under repair, including 60532 *Blue Peter* (left); 60046 *Diamond Jubilee*, built at Doncaster in 1924; 60146 *Peregrine*, built Darlington as No 2065 in 1949; 60021 *Wild Swan,* built at Doncaster as No 1869 in 1938 and B1 class 4-6-0 No 61154. Built in 1948 and withdrawn from Dundee Tay Bridge in December 1966, *Blue Peter* has subsequently been preserved. *18th September 1960*

Lichfield Trent Valley – 117 mp

Centre right: George Whale-designed, LNWR G Class 0-8-0, No 2656 built in 1910, renumbered 9079 by the LMS and 49079 by BR, is shunting part of its class 'E' down partially fitted freight. The rest of the train is in the sidings beyond the overbridge in the distance. The up gantry was repositioned 120 yards further north towards Stafford in May 1960, to allow clearance of a repositioned trailing crossover, allowing down high level branch trains to proceed northwards. *3rd June 1961*

Walsall – District Engineer's Yard

Bottom right: For a considerable time, this former LMS class 2P 4-4-0 No 40646, built at Crewe Works in 1931, was the regular Engineers' locomotive allocated by Bescot (21B) MPD. Although a Midland Railway design, first introduced in 1882, more than 100 of these locomotives were built, with modifications, by the LMS between 1928 and 1932. No 40646 was withdrawn in May 1962. *6th July 1961*

Lichfield Trent Valley Station 116¼ mp

Left: Former LMS class 5MT 4-6-0 No 45342, built in 1937 by Armstrong Whitworth, pilot to 'Jubilee' No 45582 *Central Provinces*, built in November 1934, and withdrawn in December 1962, are seen heading north with a down express. This picture shows the changing face of the West Coast Main Line at this time. The gantries to carry the overhead line equipment have been erected, though this section was not energised until January 1964. The semaphores were replaced in November 1962 by colour lights and are still controlled from the former No 1 Signal Box today. Also worth recalling is the pathway (which was closed towards the end of the 'sixties) leading off the end of the down platform to Burton Old Road, a favourite gathering place for train spotters for many years. *6th August 1961*

Lichfield Trent Valley (HL) Station

Centre left: Former LNER B1 class 4-6-0 No 61160, built by the Vulcan Foundry in 1947, heads an excursion from Lincoln St Marks to Dudley. The locomotive was allocated to Lincoln (40A) MPD. The High Level station closed in January 1965 when the service to Burton was withdrawn, but was reopened with a new platform in November 1988 when the Birmingham cross-city service from Redditch and Longbridge was extended from Lichfield City and subsequently electrified. *6th August 1961*

High Dyke – ECML

Bottom left: LNER A3 class 4-6-2 No 2546 *Donovan*, built at Doncaster Works in August 1924 and withdrawn in April 1963, as BR No 60047, is seen here approaching the north end of the 880 yards long Stoke tunnel, with a Tyne Commission Quay to Kings Cross express. The German type wind shields were fitted to many A3's from the Autumn of 1960 onwards. *7th August 1961*

Opposite page: These scenes reflect the changes occurring on the ECML around this time, as steam began to give way to diesel-electric traction. On 20th August 1960, A4 class 4-6-2 (or 'Streak' in spotter parlance) No 60034 *Lord Faringdon* climbs towards Stoke Tunnel at 101½ mp with an up express. Almost a year later, on 7th August 1961, brand new BR 'Deltic' D9007 *Pinza*, climbs the 1 in 200 gradient at 101 mp from Grantham to enter Stoke tunnel with a relief Edinburgh to London Kings Cross service. No 60034 was built at Doncaster in June 1938, carrying the name *Peregrine* and No 4903 until 1947. It took part in the 1948 inter-regional locomotive exchange trials and was withdrawn in August 1966, having finished its days in Scotland, working mainly on the Aberdeen to Glasgow expresses. The 'Deltic', built in June 1961, was withdrawn in December 1981 as No 55 007.

Lichfield Trent Valley 116mp – WCML

Above: Stanier 8F 2-8-0 No 48258 runs north with a Hartshill to Stafford ballast train consisting of loaded hopper wagons. The locomotive, which is paired here with a Fowler 3500 gallon tender fitted with coal rails, was built by the North British Locomotive Company in 1940 to a War Department order, loaned to the LMS, recalled in 1941 when given WD No 398. Its return to BR was in 1949. *2nd December 1961*

Blake Street Yard and Signal Box

Centre left: Looking East towards the station and the signal box, which closed on 4th March 1962 when intermediate block signals were installed worked from Four Oaks Signal Box, itself closed in August 1992, being replaced by a new panel in Vauxhall box. The goods and coal yard lasted until the '70s, but is now part of a residential development. This section was energised to 25kV overhead power as part of the Birmingham cross-city Lichfield TV to Redditch scheme, in October 1992. *3rd March 1962*

Littleton Sidings, nr Penkridge, Staffs

Left: The 10.15 Liverpool Lime Street to Birmingham New Street, is being worked by rebuilt 'Royal Scot' class 4-6-0 No 46115 *Scots Guardsman*. Built by the North British Locomotive Company in 1927, it was rebuilt in August 1947, withdrawn in January 1966 and subsequently preserved. This was the last locomotive of its class in service and the first to receive windshields when rebuilt. Until 1988 it was housed at the Dinting Railway Centre, but is presently at the Birmingham Railway Museum at Tyseley, undergoing restoration. *31st March 1962*

Kingsbury Station – 29¹/₂ mp

Right: These original Birmingham & Derby Junction Railway buildings on the up side were opened in August 1839. The station closed in March 1968, the buildings were demolished in 1970 and the platforms were removed in 1971. As built, the line ran from Water Orton via Whitacre. A more direct route, from Water Orton to the present Kingsbury Junction, south west of the site of the station, opened in March 1909. *14th April 1962*

Vauxhall & Duddeston Station

Centre right: The line from Aston to Sutton Coldfield was opened on 2nd June 1862. To mark the centenary, to the actual day, the Stephenson Locomotive Society ran a rail-tour. LNWR 0-8-0 No 1248, later LMS 8930 and then BR 48930 was chosen to haul this special. This locomotive, one of F W Webb's designs built at Crewe between 1901 and 1904 and later rebuilt, was withdrawn in 1962, just a few months after this event. Due to remodelling in the 1980s, the slow line platforms (right of the train) are inaccessible to and from the Birmingham direction. *2nd June 1962*

Lichfield Trent Valley – 116¹/₂ mp

Below: A down express, reporting number 1H26 from London Euston to the north-west, passes No 2 Signal Box, which closed in June 1962. It is hauled by English Electric 1 Co-Co 1 No D340, later 40.140, built at the Vulcan foundry in April 1961, withdrawn in March 1982 and cut up at Crewe works in December 1983. *8th June 1962*

Elmhurst Crossing – 118³⁄₄ mp WCML

Above: The 10.35 Workington to London Euston hauled by Ex-LMS 'Jubilee' class 4-6-0 No 45629 *Straits Settlement*, built at Crewe Works in November 1934 and withdrawn in April 1965, passes the signal box which closed along with the road crossing it protected, in August 1963. *11th June 1962*

Rugeley Trent Valley – 125³⁄₄ mp WCML

Below: Ex-LMS Class 8F 2-8-0 No 48366, built at Horwich Works in 1944, heads a freight along the up slow from Colwich Junction. The colour lights have been installed and were brought into use the following month. Energisation of the overhead line equipment followed in August 1963. *30th June 1962*

Welshpool

Above: GWR 'Manor' class 4-6-0 No 7809 *Childrey Manor*, built at Swindon Works in April 1938, was withdrawn in April 1963 and scrapped at its birthplace. Here the 'Manor' is working a local service to Oswestry. Standing on the shunt neck are an unidentified 'Manor' and a class 4300 locomotive, waiting to take over the Down 'Cambrian Coast Express'. On Saturdays in the summer this train travelled via the Abbey Foregate curve avoiding Shrewsbury station. *4th August 1962*

Lichfield City

Right: Former LMS 5MT No 42826, built at Horwich Works in November 1929 and withdrawn in September 1964, was one of a class of 245 designed by George Hughes of the Lancashire & Yorkshire Railway. They were commonly referred to by enginemen as 'Crabs'. At this time, although allocated to Newton Heath (26A) MPD, 42826 has been 'borrowed' to work this excursion from Sawley Junction, (since renamed Long Eaton) to Dudley. The high pitched angle of the cylinders was required to keep them within the loading gauge. *5th August 1962*

Pelsall Station – 9½ mp

Above: Opened by the South Staffordshire Railway in April 1849 on the Walsall to Wichnor Junction line, it closed to passengers in January 1965 and through freight in January 1984. Track lifting on this section of the line between Ryecroft Junction, Walsall and Anglesea sidings near Brownhills, was completed in 1986. *24th December 1962*

Wolverhampton High Level Station

Centre left: Looking south from the up platform (13 mp) the new Power Signal Box is externally complete, while opposite is the old LNWR No 2 Signal Box still operating the odd LNW lower quadrant arm. In the distance is No 1 Signal Box at Crane Street Junction. Multiple aspect signalling was introduced between 14th/16th August 1965, when all manual signal boxes were closed and the new installation was opened. OLE was energised between Stafford (28¼ mp) and Spring Vale Sidings (11¼ mp) on the Stour Valley line, in January 1966. *20th April 1963*

Shugborough – 128½ mp WCML

Left: Aqueduct No 140 and overbridge No 141 have been lifted and the provision of a new concrete arch completed. New 113lb flat bottomed CWR (continuous welded rail) has been laid in on concrete sleepers. Smoke plates have been attached to the new concrete arch even though steam workings would have been eliminated within approximately 3 years. OLE was energised in August and MAS had been in operation since May 1962. For a view of the site prior to improvements, see page 103. *25th April 1963*

Dundee Tay Bridge MPD (62B)

Right: Built by the North British Railway at Cowlairs Works in Glasgow in 1899, this was one of the 168 C class locomotives designed by Holmes which later became the LNER's J36 class. Twenty-five of those machines saw service overseas during the Great War and were given names associated with their military careers. One of these, NBR No 673 *Maude*, has been preserved. No 65319, pictured here, is coupled to a tender with a cab, complete with spectacles, to provide both protection from the weather and unimpaired vision for the crew when working tender first. *1st June 1963*

Centre right: A H Peppercorn, the last Chief Mechanical Engineer of the LNER, introduced his A2 class Pacifics in 1947. These were a development of the designs of his predecessor, Edward Thompson. No 60528 *Tudor Minstral* was completed at Doncaster in February 1948 as works No 2019 and first entered service allocated to Gateshead, as E528. It was withdrawn from Aberdeen Ferryhill in June 1966. *1st June 1963*

Perth MPD (63A)

Bottom right: Hawksworth-designed 0-6-0 1600 class pannier tank No 1649 is seen along with former LMS 4F 0-6-0 No 44328. Like the 1500 class pannier tank, this GWR design was built for British Railways after nationalisation. In 1957/8 two members of the 1600 class, Nos 1647 and 1649, were allocated to Helmsdale MPD (60C), north of Inverness, to work from The Mound on the Far North line, along the Dornoch branch, which had opened in June 1902. There they replaced ageing Highland Railway 0-4-4Ts, the last of which, No 55053, was withdrawn in 1957. In the BR era, relatively few locomotives moved far from where they were traditionally to be found. The appearance of pannier tanks in the far north of Scotland, were they were apparently well liked, must surely rank as one of the more unusual transfers of motive power under British Railways. No 1649 worked the last train on the Dornoch Branch, on 11th June 1960; both Nos 1647 and 1649 were condemned on 29th December 1962 and they were scrapped at Cowlairs during October 1963. *1st June 1963*

Perth MPD (63A)

Left: One of the classic Caledonian Railway 4-4-0s introduced by J F McIntosh in 1910 and developed by his successor William Pickersgill. No 54482 of the 'Dunalastair IV' class is shown withdrawn and awaiting scrapping. *1st June 1963*

Eastfield MPD, Glasgow (65A)

Centre left: Introduced by W P Reid for the North British Railway in 1914, subsequently the J37 class of the LNER and BR, these powerful 0-6-0s, of which Nos 64639 and 64580 (built at Cowlairs in 1921 and 1918 respectively) are seen here, were a superheated development of Reid's 1906 design, which became class J35 after grouping. *2nd June 1963*

Cowlairs Works, Glasgow

Bottom left: BR Standard class 4MT 2-6-0's Nos 76074 and 76100 are undergoing overhauls in the former North British workshops. The former was built at Derby in November 1956 and scrapped by G H Campbell of Airdrie, following withdrawal in October 1966. No 76100 was built at Doncaster in May 1957 and scrapped by West of Scotland Shipbreaking, following its withdrawal in August 1966. Four members of the class, all built at Horwich, have been preserved. *2nd June 1963*

Kipps MPD, Coatbridge (65E)

Opposite page centre right: Seen here are three former North British Railway locomotives, Y9 class 0-4-0ST No 68104 and two J88 class 0-6-0T's, Nos 68345 and 68350. The locomotives' wooden block buffers were fitted to prevent buffer locking on sharp curves. The centre locomotive has a tall stove-pipe chimney in contrast to the authentic original North British chimneys fitted to the other two. *3rd June 1963*

Motherwell MPD (66B)

Opposite page bottom: Former Caledonian Railway 0-6-0 locomotive No 57689 was built at St. Rollox Works in Glasgow in 1920. Introduced by W Pickersgill in 1918, this class was a development of the earlier McIntosh-designed engines. *3rd June 1963*

Parkhead MPD (65C)

Above: A general view of the shed yard reveals, from left to right, BR Standard 4-6-0 class 5MT No 73145, built at Derby in 1957, and former LMS 4-6-0 class 5's Nos 44792 (built at Horwich 1947) and 44925 (built at Crewe 1946). *2nd June 1963*

Gloucester Central

Above: BR Standard class 2-6-0 No 78009, built at Darlington in 1953, rests alongside former GWR 2-6-2T No 5184. All passenger services were concentrated here following the closure of Eastgate station in December 1975. *27th July 1963*

Pelsall

Centre left: A returning excursion from Dudley to Nottingham Midland behind former LMS 'Jubilee' class 4-6-0 No 45618 *New Hebrides*, built at Crewe Works in October 1934 and withdrawn in February 1964, approaches Ryder's Hayes Crossing, passing the 9¾ mp. The mileage was calculated from Dudley along the old South Staffs Railway. The line closed between Ryecroft Junction and Anglesea Sidings in 1984 and was lifted in 1986. *6th August 1963*

Wolverhampton Low Level

Bottom left: Approaching the North SB is a fully fitted 'class C' freight from Shrewsbury, behind former GWR 4-6-0 'Grange' class No 6874 *Haughton Grange*. Passenger services along the Chester line were diverted to the High Level station from March 1968; the Low Level station to Cannock Rd Junction closed in 1970. The new chord line direct from Bushbury, 1 mile 50 yds long, opened to Oxley in September 1983. *28th September 1963*

Opposite page top: 'Battle of Britain' class 4-6-2 No 34064 *Fighter Command*, built at Brighton in 1947, gets away from a water stop with a Talyllyn Railway special to Tywyn, which it hauled as far as Shrewsbury. *28th September 1963*

Wolverhampton High Level Station

Centre right: The original station for Wolverhampton was opened at Wednesfield by the Grand Junction Railway in July 1837. This was renamed Wednesfield Heath in November 1852. A station on the present site opened in June 1852. This was known as Wolverhampton General. The name was changed to Queen Street in September 1853 and changed again to High Level from 1st June 1885. Rebuilding, which started in February 1964 has since transformed the appearance of the station. The town's coat of arms were incorporated in the facade, which was demolished in January 1966.

Below: The train shed, looking north. No 1 platform, on the left of the picture, has a parcels office and Wymans bookstall. From platform 2 were steps to a passage which led to the GWR's Low Level Station.
Both photographs 28th September 1963

Walsall Station

Top and centre: A general view from Bridgeman Street underbridge, looking east, show-ing the five through platforms. There were also two bays at the Park Street end. The coal yard, which closed on 28th March 1964, is to the right. On the carriage clean-ing siding rests a 4-car Eastern Region EMU, brought in to train drivers for the planned electric services. Colour light signals con-trolled from Walsall PSB replaced the semaphores and Nos 2 & 3 Signal Boxes, in April 1966. The line from Bescot to Walsall was electrified from August 1966. The DMU in platform No 4, in the centre picture, is forming a service to Birmingham. Seven ser-vices once radiated from this station; these days there are only two. *26th March 1964*

Lower right: Looking east towards Ryecroft Junction from the station towards the St Pauls Street bridge, an area now covered over to form a tunnel with shops and a multi-storey car park, built above. The two slow lines, installed in 1881, (on the left) to Ryecroft Junction, were removed in January 1984. The overhead wires used by Walsall Corporation trolley buses are visible above the bridge. *3rd December 1963*

Hammerwich Station

Above: Opened by the South Staffordshire Railway in June 1849, on the line between Walsall and Wichnor Junction, the station closed when the Wolverhampton High Level to Burton-on-Trent DMU service was withdrawn in January 1965. The station's main building, on the up side, is now a private residence but the footbridge remains to take a public footpath across the singled track, used by tanker trains from Lindsay Oil Terminal to Anglesea Siding. *18th April 1964*

Birmingham New Street Station

Centre right: Queen's Drive was a private one way access road which ran through the centre of New Street station, from the junction of Navigation St with Hill Street at one end to Worcester St at the other, separating the LNWR and Midland sides of the station between platforms 6 and 7. A public right of way for pedestrians also ran across the station from Stephenson Street to Station Street, which meant that New Street had to be an open station with no ticket barriers. Removal of the war-damaged roof over the LNWR side commenced in 1948, but the overall roof on the Midland side (right), remained until rebuilding of the station started in September 1964. *14th April 1964*

Cadeby Light Railway

Bottom right: In May 1962 the late Reverend Teddy Boston purchased *Pixie*, an 0-4-0ST built by W G Bagnall at Stafford, (works no 2090 of 1919) for £75 from Staveley Minerals at Cranford in Northamptonshire, to run on his 2ft gauge line around the Rectory grounds. *Pixie* still survives, and is presently under maintenance. *18th April 1964*

Lea Green Colliery, near St Helens, Lancashire

Above: Bellerophon, an 0-6-0WT built by Richard Evans & Co Ltd in 1874, for use on their own colliery system. It was preserved and is now on the Keighley & Worth Valley Railway. *20th June 1964*

Manchester Ship Canal, Mode Wheel Shed, Salford

Above: No 63 was a Hudswell Clarke built 0-6-0T, works No 1224 of 1916. Scrapped in 1967, it was one of a class of 22 locomotives. *20th June 1964*

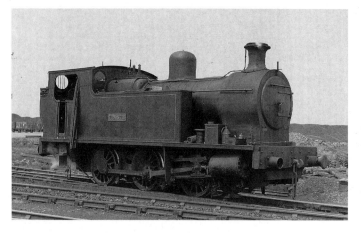

Astley Green Colliery, near Tyldesley, Lancashire

Above left: Kerr Stuart 0-6-0T No 3068 of 1917, *Francis*, has lost a buffer. It was one of a class of 10 locomotives built for the Inland Waterways Department of the War Office. Purchased by the Bridgewater Collieries for use on their extensive system west of Manchester, it survived to be fitted with a Giesl ejector before being

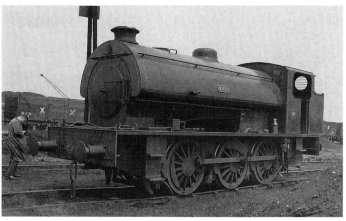

scrapped in October 1968. *Both photographs 20th June 1964*

Above right: 0-6-0ST *WHR* was built by Robert Stephenson & Hawthorn (works No 7174 of 1944) as War Department 71520. Purchased by the National Coal Board in 1947, it was one of a fleet of Austerity saddle tanks working on the colliery system centred on Walkden Yard in the two and a half decades after the war.

Haydock Collieries, Lancashire

Above: Another former Richard Evans & Co locomotive, Robert Stephenson 0-6-0T *Haydock* (works No 2309 of 1879) is now displayed at Penrhyn Castle Museum, Bangor, North Wales. *20th June 1964*

Manchester Ship Canal, Mode Wheel Shed, Salford

Above: No 30 was a Hudswell Clarke 0-6-0T, works No 663, built in 1903. There were 27 locos of this type on the Ship Canal system. It was scrapped around September 1967. *20th June 1964*

Manchester Ship Canal

Above: No 22, a Hunslet 0-6-0T, built in 1902, works number 778, one of ten such locomotives, heads a 1-coach railtour of the Manchester Ship Canal rail system. MSC Nos 31 and 32, both Hudswell Clarke locos (works numbers 679 and 680) have been preserved and are presently located on the Keighley & Worth Valley and East Lancashire Railways respectively. *20th June 1964*

Centre right: Another scene at Mode Wheel Shed, Salford. At one stage the MSC Company owned 230 miles of track, 71 steam locomotives, 2800 wagons plus ancilliary items of rolling stock. The locomotives included seven of these Kitson 0-6-0Ts – No 72 was built in 1921, works number 5357. *20th June 1964*

Lea Green Colliery

Bottom right: Newton, a Manning Wardle 0-6-0ST (works number 1504 of 1900), was one of a pair owned by Richard Evans & Co at Haydock. It was one of a number of NCB locomotives equipped with a Giesl ejector. This was a carefully proportioned multi-jet exhaust system named after its designer, the Austrian Dr Giesl-Gieslingen. The narrow rectangular shape of the chimney was a characteristic of the device, which increased the power output considerably and reduced coal consumption. The new exhaust system did not prolong the life of the locomotive for long however, as it was sold for scrap in May 1965. *20th June 1964*

Walsall (Bodleys)

Above: BR Standard class 7MT 4-6-2 No 70017 *Arrow*, running without nameplates, works a parcels train on the up fast line towards Pleck Junction, past ex-LNWR 0-8-0 No 49407 which is standing on the down fast line awaiting entry into the Midland yard. No 70017, built at Crewe in June 1951 and withdrawn in September 1966, was originally allocated to the Western Region. Following a 'Britannia' derailment at Didcot, the handrails around the smoke deflectors were replaced by grab handles to enhance the view ahead. *27th July 1964*

Dudley Port Station

Centre left: Viewed off the Sedgeley Junction loop line which was opened by the South Staffs Railway in January 1854. A passenger shuttle service was operated from here to Dudley until July 1964, when demolition of the station commenced. It was replaced by an island platform in November 1966. The girder bridge over the canal was removed in July 1970. *27th July 1964*

Bottom left: A view looking north through the station taken from the former down line, now blocked at the buffer stop in the middle distance. The LNWR signal box can be seen beyond the up platform awning, on the right of the picture. Multiple aspect signalling, controlled from Wolverhampton PSB, came in August 1965 and overhead line equipment energisation followed in October 1966. *27th July 1964*

Walsall Permanent Way yard

Right: The LNWR G2 class 0-8-0s, were a development by Capt Hewitt Pearson Montague Beames, Chief Mechanical Engineer from 1920 to 1921, of the G1 class designed by his predecessor Charles John Bowen-Cooke. No 49047, built at Crewe in 1921 as LNWR No 373, is seen here shunting a short ballast train back into the depot. The gong situated in the cess by the locomotive, provided a means of communication between a shunter or guard and the driver, during fog or falling snow when hand signals could not be seen. *5th August 1964*

Shenstone Yard

Right: These two 150ft long, 41½ ton girders, were made by the Butterley Company of Ripley in Derbyshire, for the reconstruction of underbridge No 32 on the Aston to Lichfield City line. The line was carried over a new section of the A5 road which bypassed Wall village. The services of the Crewe North and Rugby 50 ton lifting capacity steam cranes were needed to put them into position. *25th July 1964*

Wednesbury Town

Right: An experimental automatic coupler, fitted to Tube wagon No B732858, built at Darlington as part of Lot No 2867 in 1956. The wagon's capacity was 22 tons, and it is stencilled 'return to Corby'. Trains ran daily from Corby to various destinations in the Black Country, conveying steel tubes. Empty tube wagons were assembled into trains to return to Corby at Wednesbury exchange sidings. *11th August 1964*

Cosford

Left: The Shrewsbury & Birmingham Railway opened the section between Oakengates and Wolverhampton in November 1849. Here, BR Standard class 5MT 4-6-0 No 73097, built at Derby Works in December 1955 and withdrawn in May 1967, works a partly fitted freight from Oxley Sidings to Coton Hill yard, Shrewsbury. Cosford's up and down goods loops, into which any slow moving goods train could be run, were the only 'bolt' holes between Wellington and Oxley sidings. Cosford Station is still open today, served by stopping trains between Shrewsbury and Wolverhampton. It comes into its own when there is an airshow at the adjacent airfield and aerospace museum.

Below: Former GWR 4-6-0 No 6816 *Frankton Grange*, built at Swindon in December 1936, and withdrawn in July 1965, is seen working an up line freight from Shrewsbury. The signal indicates that the goods train is being diverted into the up goods loop to get it out of the way of a following passenger train. *Both 1st September 1964*

Walsall Long Street and Midland yards

Above: In this view from the old District Engineer's Office, the former LNWR Long Street Depot is to the left of the picture. To the right of the running lines, on the site of what was the extensive Midland Railway yard, is a steel terminal. 'Jubilee' 4-6-0 No 45611 *Hong Kong* passes Walsall No 1 signal box with a Derby to Birmingham parcels train. *8th September 1964*

Pleck Junction

Bottom: Here the normally double-headed 09.30 Water Orton to Wolverhampton and Wednesfield goods approaches along the up slow line headed by two Bescot-allocated ex-LNWR 0-8-0's Nos 48895 and 49430, known locally as 'Duck Eights'. This working used the Midland line, avoiding Walsall station, travelling via Lichfield Road and North Walsall junctions but M6 construction work caused this route to be severed at Birchills, and the service was thereafter diverted via Pleck Junction. *13th October 1964*

Pleck Junction Signal Box and Walsall Power Signal Box

Below: This LNWR signal box controlled the 4-track section from Walsall No 1, known locally as Bodleys. The two tracks immediately in front of the box ran to Bescot No 3, the two adjacent tracks to Bescot Curve Junction and on to Dudley, and the two tracks branching right to Darlaston Junction and Wolverhampton. The newly completed Walsall PSB, seen in the picture, was commissioned on 5th December 1965 and this led to the closure of Bescot No 3, Darlaston Junction. Walsall Nos 1, 2 and 3 – the former becoming a shunt frame – and Bescot Curve Junction SBs, lasted until April 1966. The overhead line was energised in two stages: in January 1966 from Pleck Junction to Darlaston Junction and Bescot Junction, and in August 1966 from Pleck Junction to Walsall Station. *10th September 1964*

Bescot

Above right: Before the M6 motorway dominated the skyline on the left, the reconstruction of Bescot yard is in progress. A former LMS 4F 0-6-0 is seen coming off the shed as a diesel shunter crosses from the down Grand Junction line to the up side. No 3 (nearest the camera) and No 2 signal boxes can also be seen. *13th October 1964*

Bescot Curve Junction Signal box

Above left: Almost obscured by construction work for the M6 motorway, this box was between Pleck Junction, Walsall and Wednesbury Town on that part of the South Staffs Railway which opened on 1st May 1850. The box itself closed in April 1966. The lines in the foreground rise up from Bescot No 3 Signal Box and the route from Pleck Junction through to Round Oak, meet outside the box and under the M6, were mothballed in 1992, though are presently still in existence . *15th October 1964*

Walsall No 1

Top: Another view of the ex-LNWR 0-8-0's Nos 48895 and 49430, setting back on the up slow to attach additional wagons. Note both locomotives have tender cabs and their cab sides display diagonal yellow lines denoting that they were not permitted south of Crewe on lines with overhead electrification, due to the height of the locomotives. A fogman's hut stands adjacent to the gantry, which carries No 1's home signals and No 2 distants, for both down slow and down fast lines. *13th October 1964*

Bescot Station

Above: Complete reconstruction of the station, which originally opened in November 1847, and the marshalling yard – whose up side opened December 1881 and down sorting sidings in October 1892 – is in progress. No 2 Signal Box, in the picture, was closed with the introduction of MAS controlled from Walsall PSB, in December 1965. *15th October 1964*

Walsall Gas Works

Centre right: This was situated on the down side of the south Staffordshire line between Walsall No 1 Signal Box and Pleck Junction. Rail traffic ceased in 1969 following closure of the Works in August of the previous year. Peckett 0-4-0ST, works No 597 of 1895, which spent its entire life here, shunts the gas sidings. This locomotive was cut up on site by Cashmore's of Great Bridge, in July 1970. An older Peckett (1895), acquired from Cannock Lodge Colliery at Bloxwich, was kept as a spare. A 4-wheeled Sentinel, No 9632 of 1957, could also be found here at one period. *15th October 1964*

Great Bridge North – Eagle Crossing

Bottom right: Parked in J.Cashmore's scrapyard, silently awaiting the cutter's torch, are 'Coronation' class 4-6-2's Nos 46254 *City of Stoke-on-Trent*, built at Crewe in September 1946, and 46245 *City of London*. The latter was also built at Crewe, but in June 1943, and with a streamlined casing, which it retained until August 1947. Both locomotives were withdrawn from service in September 1964. *11th November 1964*

Birmingham New St Station, South End

Left: Reconstruction is well in hand. No 1 Signal Box is still in use but was to close with the opening of the PSB and introduction of MAS in January 1966. At platform No 3 is a class 40, D306, later 40 106, built by Robert Stephenson & Hawthorns Ltd in November 1960. Withdrawn in April 1983, it was sold into preservation and is now on the Nene Valley Railway, carrying the name *Atlantic Conveyor.* The overhead line electrification between Spring Vale and Adderley Park was energised in October 1966. *20th May 1965*

Bescot Motive Power Depot (21F)

Below centre: A general view of the shed, which was opened in 1892 and closed on 28th March 1966. At the time of writing, it still stands. *10th June 1965*

Walsall Permanent Way Yard

Opposite page top: The Walsall District Engineer was responsible for the maintenance of all the former LMS lines in the West Midlands from Stafford South to Rugby and from Barnt Green in the west to Tamworth in the east. The former GWR lines in the area had their own District Engineer based at Wolverhampton Low Level. The two districts were amalgamated to form the Birmingham Division in 1966. In the foreground is the former LMS class 2MT 2-6-0 No 46522, in lined green livery, which replaced the ex-Midland 4-4-0 (see page 133), as the Walsall depot's regular engine. *10th June 1965*

Walsall Station

Opposite page centre: This was the fifth station built at Walsall. Planned by the LNWR but opened in November 1923 by the LMSR, it was situated in Park Street on the corner with Station Street, a site now occupied by a Marks & Spencer store. The booking hall was rectangular, 70ft wide and 32 ft deep, panelled entirely in oak and incorporated a bookstall. Demolition took place in 1978 and the large ornate portico was rescued for eventual display somewhere in the town. An entrance to the current (sixth) station was opened within the Saddlers Shopping Centre in July 1980. *2nd June 1965*

Seaton Station

Opposite page bottom: Situated on the Rugby to Peterborough East line, this was the junction for two branches, one to Uppingham and the other to Luffenham on the former Midland, Manton Junction to Stamford route. The passenger service to Uppingham ceased in June 1960. Both the Rugby to Peterborough and Seaton to Luffenham lines closed in June 1966. BR Standard class 2MT 2-6-2T No 84013, built at Crewe in October 1953 and withdrawn in January 1966, stands in the down platform with the 12.38 push-pull train to Stamford via Luffenham. *12th June 1965*

Norton Junction, No 3 SB and yard

Above: These extensive sidings were off the South Staffs line at Norton Junction between Pelsall and Brownhills. To the right is No 3 Signal Box which controlled the branch to East Cannock Junction on the Ryecroft Junction to Rugeley Trent Valley line, over which vast quantities of coal from the Cannock Chase collieries came for marshalling and onward transit from here. The sidings were closed in 1981 and lifted in 1984. *19th June 1965*

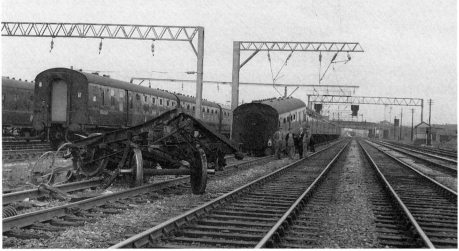

Walsall Shunt Frame (formerly No 1 SB)

Centre left: Empty stock from the Midland yard, for Wolverhampton High Level, was released on to the up fast line. It is believed that the derailment occurred when a pair of facing points were reversed between the bogies of the rear vehicle, BSK M27006; this being the result. *28th July 1965*

Walsall Shunt Frame

Left: A special of fly ash from Ocker Hill power station at Wednesbury to Harpenden approaches from Pleck Junction along the down slow line, headed by BR Standard 2-10-0 class 9F No 92213, built at Swindon Works in October 1959 and withdrawn just seven years later in November 1966. Disposal was to J McWilliam at Shettleston. The attached BR.1G tender could carry 7 tons of coal and 5000 gallons of water. The lamp bracket, originally positioned on top of the smokebox door in front of the chimney, has been moved to beneath the smokebox door number plate, removing the need for the train crew to climb up, dangerously close to overhead line equipment, in order to place or remove a lamp from the bracket. The OLE insulators are wrapped in plastic; this stretch between Pleck Junction and Walsall Station was not energised until August 1966. *4th August 1965*

Birmingham New Street Station

Above: Part of the rebuilding at the station involved the removal of a 90 ton steel girder from the Midland side, at the Worcester Street end of Queen's Drive, by Willesden Depot's 75 ton steam crane and a 50 ton road crane.
8th August 1965

Uphill & Bleadon Station

Above: The Somerset Railway Museum was located at this closed station on the original Bristol & Exeter route. This selection was on the up platform. One of the larger items was Cardiff Railway No 5, an 0-4-0ST built by Kitson's in 1898, (works number 3799). Upon closure it eventually found its way to the GWR Society at Didcot. *12th September 1965*

Highbridge Station (S&D Joint)

Below: The Somerset Central Rlwy opened the line between Highbridge and Glastonbury in August 1854. By 1861 the line had been extended to Burnham-on-Sea. Highbridge Station had five platforms, in No 3 bay is ex-LMS 2-6-2T No 41307 with an Evercreech Junction service. The Burnham extension closed May 1963 and the line to Evercreech in January 1966. *15th September 1965*

Wolverhampton (HL) North Junction

Top left: The extension of tracks beyond the former GWR Herbert Street Goods Depot to form a new junction with the Stour Valley line (at 13 miles 704 yds from Birmingham New Street and 143 miles 1148 yds from Paddington) was completed on 5th June 1966. The new line and the GWR route to Shrewsbury was electrified as far as Oxley sidings in May 1972. This enabled the GWR line from Wolverhampton Low Level station to Cannock Road Junction to be closed on 4th March 1968, from which date all Shrewsbury line train services were transferred to the High Level station. A new bay platform, No 1C, was eventually brought into use to handle some of the additional DMUs brought into the High Level station by these changes. *24th May 1966*

Wolverhampton Low Level

Opposite page, top right: Ex-GWR 'Special' saloon No 9118, now a 40 ton second open, in the Carriage Shed. Stencilled below the tail lamp is the warning that it was 'Not to run over the eastern or western valleys, north of Saltney Junction and between Little Mill Junction and Maindee Junction'. *23rd June 1966*

Opposite page, centre: Standing on the up goods line, bounded by the station and the carriage shed, is former GWR 0-6-0PT No 8767. This Oxley (84B) MPD-allocated locomotive has had all its identification plates removed. *10th June 1966*

Birmingham Central Goods Depot (Worcester Wharf)

Opposite page, bottom: Viewed from the top floor of Rail House, now Quayside Tower, in Broad Street, work on Britain's largest Post Office sorting office has begun beyond the goods shed, above the multi-storey car park in the centre of the picture. The Midland Railway opened the Worcester Wharf Depot on 1st July 1887 at the end of the branch from Church Road Junction; it closed in 1967 though demolition was delayed until 1973 when work on the LMR HQ building, Stanier House, began. *21st February 1967*

Birmingham Central Goods offices

This page, top right: Built by the Midland Railway in 1892, this triangular shaped building bounded by Suffolk Street, Allport Street and Holliday Street was demolished in the Autumn of 1967 to make way for the Queensway elevated road section to Holloway Head. *5th August 1967*

Lichfield City Station

Below: The station, with its 280 yard island platform between Nos 1 and 2 Signal Boxes. No 2 SB, demolished in March 1974, is the one in the foreground. The scissors crossings in the centre of both the up and down platform lines were removed at that time. The up and down through lines, next to the platform lines, were taken out of use in March 1991 as part of the rationalisation of track in connec-

tion with the route electrification through to Lichfield Trent Valley Station. No 1 SB closed on 12th October 1992. *20th August 1967*

Baptist End Halt

Above: The Old Hill to Dudley line opened on 1st March 1898 and closed on 15th June 1964. The tracks have gone, ballast sold, but platforms and vandalised shelters remain. *3rd March 1968*

Birmingham Central Goods Depot

Left: The Goods Shed still stands, along with the signalling, but the tracks have gone. The site was eventually cleared for building the new LMR Headquarters, 'Stanier House', early in 1973. *4th April 1968*

Five Ways Station

Centre left: This station opened on 1st July 1885 on the West Surburban line from Birmingham New Street to Kings Norton. It was closed temporarily in October 1944 and permanently from November 1950. A new station has been built on the site and opened on 7th May 1978 as part of the Cross-City service. The track bed to the right was that of the former Church Road Junction to Birmingham Central Goods branch, opened in July 1887 and closed in 1967. The banking of expresses from Birmingham New Street up a 1 in 80 gradient through five tunnels (Suffolk Street, Holliday Street, Canal, Granville Street and Bath Row) was a regular occurrence on this stretch of line. The banking engines dropped off at Church Road Junction where they crossed over to the up line to return to New Street. (See page 84). *4th May 1968*

Aberystwyth

Below: Former GWR 600mm gauge locomotive No 7 *Owain Glyndower*, one of only three steam locomotives to be operated by BR after the end of standard gauge steam in August 1968, until bought in March 1989 for £306,500 by the Brecon Mountain Railway. No 7 stands in the former Carmarthen line bay platform. *10th July 1968*

Soho and Winson Green Station

Above: Here, engineers clear lineside rubbish onto a ballast train, as it travels wrong line on the up main through the station. When the service on this section of the former GWR main line north of Birmingham was reduced to only a DMU shuttle, the by now unstaffed stations were quickly vandalised. Closure of the Snow Hill to Wolverhampton Low Level line stations took place from 6th March 1972, but it is expected that this trackbed will be covered by the Midland Metro Line One route between these centres, in due course. *8th August 1969*

Bilston Central Signal box

Centre left: This signal box closed on 26th January 1969, but a sporadic service of DMUs continued to rattle past the vandalised remains until March 1972. *31st August 1969*

Swan Village South Junction

Centre right: The service from Dudley to Snow Hill, which joined the main line at Swan Village South Junction, ceased in June 1964. The Great Bridge to Swan Village line closed completely on 1st January 1968 and the signal box closed in November of that year. *12th September 1969*

Winson Green Goods Depot

Below: Built by the GWR during the 1930s with government financial assistance, this large depot off Boulton Road closed not

long after this photograph was taken. A light industrial estate is now here. The electrified former LNWR line between Soho East Junction and Perry Barr North Junction is in the background. *1st April 1970*

Lightmoor Junction, Telford

Left: Coal trains to Ironbridge power station still pass through this Junction, using the line from Madeley Junction, on the Wolverhampton to Shrewsbury route, seen on the left of the picture. The line north to Wellington, on the right, and south of the power station to Much Wenlock and on to Craven Arms closed in July 1962 to passenger services. Lightmoor Junction Signal Box closed in May 1995 and the line to Ironbridge is now singled. *7th July 1970*

Trench Crossing and Station

Centre: The Shropshire Union Railway opened the Wellington to Stafford line in June 1849. Passenger services ceased in September 1964. The line closed completely between Newport and Stafford in August 1966, and Donnington to Newport in November 1969. The line between Wellington and the large Ordnance depot at Donnington was singled in 1971 and has since closed. *7th July 1970*

Nuneaton Abbey Street Station

Left: The line opening to Hinckley in January 1862 was from the LNWR station (TV). Whitacre to Nuneaton (Midland) opened in November 1864. A new station, replacing the original beyond the bridge, opened in September 1873 as Midland, but it was renamed Abbey Street in June 1924. Passenger services ceased to call at this station from March 1968, diverting via Trent Valley station. Closure of Abbey Junction and Midland Junction came in February 1992 and tracklifting between the two was completed in September 1993. *16th August 1970*

Tyseley DMU Sidings

Above: BR Standard class 7MT 4-6-2 No 70000 *Britannia*, the locomotive after which the whole class was often referred, was built at Crewe Works in January 1951. It was named by the Minister of Transport at a ceremony at Marylebone Station on 30th January. Withdrawn in May 1966 from Newton Heath depot and placed into store, it is seen here *en route* from Redhill to Kidderminster for restoration to running order on the preserved Severn Valley Railway. Restoration to BR main line running standards was completed at Carnforth during 1991. *22nd March 1971*

Hednesford No 3 Signal Box

Centre right: An LNWR-type box, opened in 1923, it was still operating elevated lower quadrant arms, at this time. Its eventual demise came with the closure of West Cannock Colliery in December 1977. The up home signal post, beside the box, was 35ft high, to give drivers approaching on a curve and a rising gradient, as early a sighting as possible. The distant signal on this post was controlled from Hednesford No 2 Signal Box. Note the string of MGR wagons on the pit siding. *7th September 1971*

Birmingham Snow Hill Station

Right: What a sorry state! Platform Nos 5 and 7 and the 4-track bed between them are in use as a car park. The station, which had opened in 1852, was not given the name Snow Hill until 1858. Although through expresses had finished in 1968, a bay at the north end of the station dealt with the remaining daily services to Langley Green and Wolverhampton Low Level, until they ceased, in March 1972. The 'new' Snow Hill Station rose from the ashes to open with services to Stratford and Leamington in October 1987. Services over the reinstated tracks to Smethwick West are due to start in late 1995. *15th October 1971*

Shifnal

Above: A GWR shunting signal of a type introduced in 1915. *23rd June 1972*

Banbury Sidings

Top: Manually operated Crane No 403 was built at Swindon Works by the GWR in November 1929. It bore a plate which read, 'Return to Divisional Engineer Shrewsbury at Coleham Depot'. Here the crane is being used by the Carriage and Wagon Department in the up sidings, to change wheel sets. *28th October 1971*

Lightmoor Junction

Above left: Diesel electric No D1812, built by Brush in February 1965, and later renumbered 47331, hauls an empty MGR train from Buildwas Power Station. *1st June 1972*

Wilnecote Station

Above: This station was opened in May 1842 as Wilnecote and Fazeley by the Birmingham & Derby Joint Railway. It was renamed plain Wilnecote in 1904. These buildings, on the down platform, were demolished in 1973. The booking office, of more recent design, faces the A5 road on ground level. Wilnecote enjoys a good passenger service, considering how close it is to Tamworth. High Level *4th September 1972*

Spon Lane

Centre right: Underbridge No 23 on the Stour Valley line, where canal bridges canal, the railway bridges one of the canals and the M5 motorway bridge crosses over the lot. Looking towards Sandwell and Dudley (formerly Oldbury) station. The railway is the main Birmingham to Wolverhampton Stour Valley Line; the canals are the Birmingham and its later extension. *4th September 1972*

West Bromwich Signal Box

Right: It was not all that common to see a signal box on a platform, as seen here, at the north end of the up platform. Closed before the local passenger service finished in March 1972, it became the target of vandals until demolished soon after this photograph was taken. The long proposed Birmingham to Wolverhampton 'Midland Metro Line One' tramway, on the route of the former GWML, north from Snowhill, may yet bring rails back to this location. *5th May 1973*

Wellington (Shropshire) Station

Top: A view towards No 3 Signal Box, which closed, along with No 4 SB, on 30th September 1973. Only the former No 2 survives today, out of the four which once served Wellington. *15th May 1973*

Banbury Junction

Above: A view northwards with the track bed of the former GCR line to Woodford Halse, opened in 1900 and closed in 1966, veering off to the right, opposite the signal box. *10th July 1974*

Hollinswood Signal Box

Right: Work in connection with the building of the M54 motorway is going on around the signal box. The extensive marshalling yard has already disappeared. A new station, called Telford Central, was opened near this spot on 12th May 1986. This view looks towards Oakengates. *10th May 1978*

Lichfield Trent Valley Station

Below: When I heard that 25kV AC electric locomotive No 86 207 was to receive the name *City of Lichfield*, I approached the City Council with the suggestion that plaques bearing the Arms of the city should also be affixed to the locomotive. The City Council and British Rail agreed, and the plaques were produced by a firm at Stratford-upon-Avon, from where I collected them on 26th February and conveyed them to Willesden Depot, for fixing prior to the naming ceremony at Lichfield Trent Valley Station, which was performed by Lady Leonora, Countess of Lichfield. *2nd March 1981*

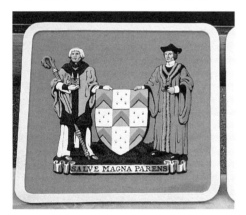

Crewe Station

Centre right: Class 47 No 47 076 *City of Truro*, built at Crewe in February 1965 and formerly D1660, passes on the up through with a pre-fabricated track train, off the Chester line. The name plates of this locomotive were presented to the City of Truro in 1989, following transfer of the name to HST power car 43 192. *9th July 1984*

Right: AC electric locomotive No 86 207 *City of Lichfield*, pauses at Crewe with a Euston to Liverpool via Birmingham service. It still bears the crest of the City of Lichfield which had been affixed some six years earlier, as described above. This locomotive was built in October 1965 (as E3179) by the English Electric Company at Newton-le-Willows, and was the fifth to bear a name connected to the City. South Staffordshire Railway No 4 of 1849 bore the name *Lichfield*, while LNWR 'Dreadnought' class No 641 of 1888, LNWR 'Experiment' class No 165 of 1906 and LMSR Pacific No 6250 (BR 46250) of 1944 all carried the name *City of Lichfield*, the latter until withdrawal in September 1964. *16th July 1987*

Stoke-on-Trent, Cockshut Sidings

Above: The sidings situated north of the station and PSB on the up side were closed and the signal box demolished in 1987. The tracks were subsequently lifted. With the move from wagon load to block trains and the reduction of the amount of shunting involved, plus the decline in the number of works and private sidings served by goods trains, many locations such as this have been rendered redundant in the last 30 years or so. *11th January 1984*

Duddeston Carriage Shed – Grand Junction line

Above: Electric Multiple Units (EMUs) Nos 310.048 and 310.037 were housed in this disused shed, under police guard, on the 21st March 1985, after a passenger was murdered in '048, en route between Northampton and Rugby, the day before. Dewiring of the sidings was completed on 19th February 1987 and they were lifted by contractors during April. Gales blew down the shed wall (left) in April 1989 and complete demolition followed. *11th January 1984*

Rugby – Locomotive Testing Station

Left: The exterior of Rugby's famous Locomotive Testing Station, not long before it was demolished in October 1984. A joint LNER & LMSR enterprise, it was started in 1937, suspended during the war, and opened October 1948 with A4 No 60007 *Sir Nigel Gresley* in attendance. *1st August 1984*

Rugby – Locomotive Testing Station

Above: An interior scene with all machinery and rollers removed and the test bed area flooded with red hydraulic fluid and water. The last locomotive testing took place in 1965 and the machinery was dismantled in 1970. Compare this desolate view with that on page 22. *1st August 1984*

Crewe South Junction

Left: Major track and signalling remodelling, costing £14.3 million, was undertaken between 2nd June and 21st July. At this time, and on target, the new south junction has been laid in on hardwood timbers using 113 lb rail, and the drilling gangs are busy. This view is looking north between the down and up fast line ladder junction, adjacent to the carriage shed. *14th June 1985*

Stafford Motive Power Depot

Above: With an allocation reduced to only nine locomotives, '5C' closed in July 1965. The building remained empty until October 1987, when refurbishment began the transformation into light industrial units. *26th March 1986*

Birmingham Moor Street

Above: Site of the former Didcot to Chester through route into Snow Hill Station. Work commenced in the autumn of 1984 to construct a new Moor Street Station which opened on 28th September 1987, following closure of the old station two days before. The first scheduled DMU services into the new Snow Hill Station began on 5th October 1987. *4th August 1986*

Nottingham Station

Right: An empty MGR train passes the former Midland Railway Goods Warehouse, headed by a pair of class 20 1,000 hp Bo-Bo diesel locomotives. Nos 20 185 (originally D8185) and 20 210 (originally D8310) were both built by English Electric in 1967. Demolition of the imposing building behind them began seven months later, in March 1988. Both locomotives were cut up by MC Metal Processing of Glasgow, in August 1994 and November 1993 respectively. *19th August 1987*

Birmingham Moor Street

Right: The old GWR station on the left of the picture opened on 1st July 1909 and was closed on 26th September 1987. The new station opened on the rebuilt line to the new Snow Hill station on 28th September 1987, although the first official public trains did not run through to Snow Hill until 5th October 1987. The site occupied by the car park was formerly the large Moor Street Goods Station, opened in January 1914 to handle all traffic previously dealt with at Bordesley Depot. Only the livestock, for which extensive cattle pens were built, remained at Bordesley. The depot closed in November 1972. The old station has been mothballed at the request of Birmingham City Council, for possible museum development. *25th September 1987*

Top left: The famous 'Orient Express' train visits the town, headed by class 47 Co-Co diesel No 47 484 *Isambard Kingdom Brunel*, built at Crewe works in 1965 as D1662. The locomotive was in lined green livery, with a raised logo on the cab side.
19th December 1987

Rugby – 82 mp WCML

Centre left: AC electric locomotive No 86 231 *Starlight Express* (originally built at Doncaster in November 1965 as E3126) passes under the marooned former Great Central Railway 'birdcage' bridge south of Rugby Station, with the 12.26 departure for London Euston. No 86 231 was named in October 1984. This was the location where I took many of my favourite photographs in the days of steam. *17th February 1988*

Changing Stations

Below, centre: British Rail and West Midlands Passenger Transport Executive logo's on display at Blake Street station on the Birmingham to Lichfield line.

Below right: The South Staffordshire Railway opened a passenger service between Walsall and Cannock in February 1858, extending to Hednesford and Rugeley in November 1859. Local services ceased between Walsall and Rugeley in January 1965, but were reinstated as far as Hednesford in April 1989. The newly constructed Bloxwich North Station, between Bloxwich and Ladywood, opened in October 1990, displaying the logo-type of 'Centro' – the organisation that had taken over responsibility from the WMPTE, for supporting local rail services in the area, as from 31st January of that year.
Both photos 14th October 1990

Rugeley Station – 124¼ mp WCML

Below: Two newly-constructed 5000 hp Bo-Bo AC electric locomotives, Nos 90 006 and 90 009, travel along the up fast line of the WCML from Crewe to Willesden DED (Diesel & Electric Depot), to take up duties. *7th September 1988*

POSTSCRIPT

In this book I have tried to reflect on how the railways of Britain have changed over the years when I was actively involved in the industry as an employee of British Railways. It was my interest in railways that led me to go to work on the railway and that interest has of course been sustained in the years since I retired from the job. As this book entered the final stages of production before publication, it occurred to both myself and my publishers that a good way to round it off, would be to go out and record a selection of images of the current scene on some of the lines which have featured elsewhere on these pages, with particular reference to the motive power which can now be seen on these tracks.

I have, of course, not been able to record on film the biggest change of all to effect the railways of Britain in 1994. This was the passing of the Railways Act, which became law, without a hint of irony, on 1st April of that year. This signalled the beginning of the privatisation of the railways of Britain and the end of British Rail as we have come to love or loathe it. New names such as 'Railtrack' and those of the train operating companies have begun to enter the railway vocabulary. Whether this is the beginning of a new era of prosperity and high investment or just a cynical excuse by government to get out of subsidising the railway, that will lead to mass closures and the replacement of a great co-ordinated national asset by a fragmented collection of private fiefs, time alone will tell.

The railway has never stood still, it is always changing. Sometimes the changes are dramatic, like the end of steam, or the electrification of a stretch of line, others are almost imperceptible and gradual, like the mechanisation of track maintenance. Traffic flows are lost and new ones are gained, lines and stations close whilst others are opened or revived. This is what keeps the subject so interesting.

The next fifty years will no doubt be as intriguing as the half century I have had the pleasure of observing and recording, and which I hope you will have enjoyed sharing with me in the pages of this book.

Stafford Station

Above: A loaded Merry Go Round (MGR) train for Ironbridge Power Station runs through on the up fast line at Stafford station prior to crossing over to continue along the Grand Junction line to Bushbury Junction, behind diesel locomotive 56 092, built at Doncaster in 1981. The first batch of 30 class 56 locomotives was built by Electroputere in Romania and introduced into service in 1976. Some members of the class have already been withdrawn. The coal trains to Ironbridge are now virtually the only freight traffic on the Shrewsbury to Wolverhampton line, from which they diverge at Madeley Junction. *17th August 1994*

Walsall (Albert Street Bridge)

Right: Class 58s Nos 58 013 and 58 035 with an empty MGR train from Ironbridge Power Station to the East Midlands. *11th September 1993*

Walsall (Albert Street Bridge)

Left: One of British Rail's latest diesel freight locomotives is the Brush-built 3100 hp Co-Co class 60. No 60 086 *Schiehallion* heads towards Rye-croft Junction with an empty MGR train from Rugeley Power Station to the East Midlands, having run round at Bescot Yard. See page 146 (lower photograph) reference the multi-storey car park, and the slow line. *11th August 1994*

Polesworth – 106¼ mp WCML

Below: A Rail Freight Distribution sector electric class 90, No 90 149, heads a freight-liner working from Manchester Trafford Park to Wembley International through the up slow platform line at Polesworth. The concrete base between the tracks is all that remains of the Polesworth signal box which closed as recently as July 1990. The station became unstaffed from October 1972. *13th August 1994*

Rugeley Station

Left: Plasser & Theurer 07-16 Universal tamping and lining machine No DR 73252 passes through Rugeley station up the Ryecroft Junction branch. This machine, one of a large fleet owned by Railtrack, packs the ballast under the sleepers and aligns the track – essential parts of track maintenance, which were formerly part of the responsibility of the permanent way gangs. These local gangs, based at the stations, were each tasked with maintaining their own section of track and also had to look after fences, drains, vegetation and even the control of wildlife, such as rabbits, on their stretch. *13th May 1992*

Bescot Stadium Station.

Right: Some examples of the first generation of modern traction still soldier on. Vintage DMU 'Heritage set' 117 331, made up of coaches 51340, 51375 and 51381, forms the 10.30 Birmingham New Street to Walsall, substituting for an EMU. This set was transferred to Tyseley from Network SouthEast (NSE) Thames at Reading and still carries the NSE logotype and livery. *11th August 1994*

Birmingham Snow Hill Station

Centre left: 'Centro' Sprinter unit No 150 128, made up of coaches 52128 and 57128, stands in No 4 platform with the 09.55 to Leamington. Those who criticised the run down and eventual closure of the former GWR station in Birmingham in the 1960s and '70s were vindicated when a new station was built on the site in the 1980s. Even changes for the worst can be redressed in time. *19th August 1994*

Birmingham New Street Station

Centre right: Class 166 Turbo Express unit No 166 212, made up of coaches 58133, 58612 and 58112, leaves the north end of No 8 platform with the 09.01 to London Paddington via Stourbridge Junction and Worcester Shrub Hill. Though not as prepossessing as a 'King' or a 'Castle' on a long rake of coaches (see page 73), it is pleasing to record that through services from Birmingham to Paddington have been resumed. *19th August 1994*

Right: BREL class 158 Express DMU No 158 850 leaves No 5 platform with the 10.37 to Shrewsbury while the 10.34 to Manchester Piccadilly via Stoke-on-Trent stands in No 6 platform, worked by sister unit No 158 747. *19th August 1994*

Birmingham New Street

Top left: EMU No 323 213 enters Birmingham New Street Station with a Longbridge to Lichfield Trent Valley service. The electrification of the cross city line is a reflection of the growing importance and popularity of rail as an alternative to the car for commuters in the West Midlands.
19th August 1994

Atherstone – 102¼ mp WCML

Top right: Though the route is not as important as it was in past decades, through services still run from Euston to Holyhead on the tracks of the 'Irish Mail'. The 08.53 London Euston to Holyhead passes through Atherstone worked by an High Speed Train (HST), with power car 43 029 leading and 43 034 at the rear. *13th August 1994*

Left: Driving Van Trailer (DVT) No 82 101 *Wembley Depot Quality Approved,* heads the 10.08 Crewe to London Euston through Atherstone Station, propelled at the rear by electric locomotive No 87 004 *Britannia.* DVT No 82 101 was the first of its class to receive a name, at a ceremony at Wembley InterCity Depot on the 25th June 1994. Compare this view with that on page 108 showing Atherstone's elevated signal box. It was replaced by a BR designed box which in turn closed in July 1990. The station became unstaffed in October 1972. *13th August 1994*

Tail Lamp

Left: The common oil tail lamp had been used on the railways for a very long time but the decade prior to 1985 saw its gradual replacement by a modern battery operated model. Like brake van side lights, the oil lamp was due to disappear by the end of the 1980s. This photograph was taken on Stafford Station and shows some of the old soldiers lined up and ready for duty. It seems that everything on the railway is subject to change, from the locomotive at the front to the lamp at the tail. *19th June 1985*